RECEIVE SURRENDER TRUST ALLOW RECEIVE SURRENDER TRUST ALLOW RECEIVE SURRENDER TRUST ALLOW

S·T·A·R

PHILOSOPHY

accept
thyself
as divine

S.T.A.R. Series
Book 1

ALSO BY NINA BROWN

Return of Love to Planet Earth: Memoir of a Reluctant Visionary

The Fascinated Observer: A Guide to Embodying S.T.A.R. Philosophy

S·T·A·R

SURRENDER TRUST ALLOW RECEIVE SURRENDER TRUST ALLOW RECEIVE SURRENDER TRUST ALLOW RECEIVE

PHILOSOPHY

accept
thyself
as divine

THIRD EDITION

NINA BROWN

FOREWORD BY BRAHMARSHI PATRIJI

SANTA FE, NEW MEXICO

Published by Cauda Pavonis
PO Box 32445
Santa Fe, NM 87594
CaudaPavonisPub.com

Published in the United States of America

Project development/Editor: Ja-lene Clark
Editors: Jo Ann Deck, Joanne Sprott
Interior and cover design: Ja-lene Clark
Interior and cover production: Janice St. Marie
Illustrations: Ja-lene Clark
Author photo: "Nina Brown Emerging from James F. Jereb's painting *Infinity II— Love,*" Mindscape Portrait by photographer Lorran Meares, enlight-10.com
Art credit: Pages 18 and 76, *Infinity II—Love,* painting by James F. Jereb, PhD © 2010
Logo: Tammy Mabra

Publisher's Cataloging-in-Publication Data

Names: Brown, Nina, 1944- author.
Title: S.T.A.R. philosophy : accept thyself as divine / Nina Brown ; foreword by Brahmarshi Patriji.
Description: Third edition. | Santa Fe, New Mexico : Cauda Pavonis, [2017] | Series: S.T.A.R. series ; book 1 | "Originally published as S.T.A.R.: a now state of being"--Title page verso.
Identifiers: ISBN: 978-0-9826769-1-2 | LCCN: 2016919862
Subjects: LCSH: Spiritual life. | Self (Philosophy) | Self-consciousness (Awareness) | Self psychology. | Self-realization. | Perfection. | Excellence. | Metacognition. | Ascension of the soul.
Classification: LCC: BF697 .B76 2017 | DDC: 158.1--dc23

To James F. Jereb, PhD
who listened and trusted his inner voice,
"S.T.A.R. is to be known on the planet."

ACKNOWLEDGMENTS

Appreciation and gratitude are extended to the star seed pioneers, who trusted me when I asked that they help create the first S.T.A.R. clinics: Ananda Mayi, René Fugitt, Dr. Amit Goswami, Julie Gullick-Wiley, William Henry, Crisostomo Jacinto, Tammy Mabra, J. Lynch, DC, Wendy Martin, MD, Randolph Masters, PhD, Jayne Mason, Matthew Reifslager, Christa J. Obuchowski, Debbie M. Simerl, Raquel Spencer, Norma Tarango, Dr. Vladimir Turek, CJ Walker and Robert Winn.

I acknowledge the artistic mastery of both Tammy Mabra, for the original book image used to design the cover and the S.T.A.R. logo and James F. Jereb, PhD, for having the visionary awareness to paint the particles of creation in *Infinity II —Love*.

Alison James changed the course of my destiny by introducing me to Ja-lene Clark, my original publisher, who then asked me to write this book—deep gratitude.

Thank you, Ja-lene Clark, for inspiring the creation of this book and for helping the words it contains to dance.

After publication of the first edition of S.T.A.R., Jennifer Elsner, Chelsea Fullerton and Michelle Martello were instrumental in shaping my disparate thoughts and visions into the clarity now radiating from my new website and message.

The miracle of meeting Kristy Sweetland has blossomed into our next book, *The Fascinated Observer: A Guide to Embodying S.T.A.R. Philosophy*, which she crafted so elegantly.

I am enormously grateful to Debbie Jacobson and Marleen Koning, who brought me such delight as they extended my dream by opening up S.T.A.R. Circle Book Clubs in different parts of the world.

Yvonne van Buren Schele, Kathleen Dale Byrnes, Agnès Hémery, Barbara Jacksa, Merita Bat Shoshan, Joanne Sprott and Alison Stratman are gratefully acknowledged for spreading the S.T.A.R. philosophy by means of their articles, which share their unique experiences applying S.T.A.R.

Appreciation is felt for Eugene Ahn, MD, Cara Cargill, René Fugitt, Laurian Lucretia, Sydney McCain and Rhoda Mitchell, who are or will be integrating the S.T.A.R. philosophy into their books.

Sam Berne, OD, Jenneken Berends, Sameeta Nanjiani, Brahmarshi Patriji, Tammi Rager and Pradeep Vijay are radiant beings opening doors for the S.T.A.R. philosophy to flow out into the world.

And finally, I want to send love and gratitude to every sweet, wonderful soul who has had the courage to reach out to touch S.T.A.R. and share it with their loved ones.

CONTENTS

APPLYING THE WISDOM OF S.T.A.R. IN EVERYDAY SITUATIONS—134

LIVE EVERY DAY AS A SACRED MOMENT—172

EMANCIPATION PROCLAMATION OF HUMAN DIVINITY—176

FOREWORD

We are all currently in an Age of Mass Enlightenment.

We are in an Age where Seekers of Truth, Seekers of Everlasting Peace and Seekers of Global Harmony are grandly outnumbering Non-Seekers.

We are in an Age with numerous Perfect Masters donning a physical body to help the whole of humanity toward Stellar and Dimensional Enlightenment. Nina Brown's life and teachings are a great addition to the Galaxy of Stellar Masters.

Surrendering Ourselves to Ourselves, surrendering our Personality-Self to our Universal-Self, trusting the whole process and allowing the effects thereof on the Personality-Self, and receiving beauty, grace, energy and light into our Earth-Self is the crux of the whole phenomenon of Cosmic Enlightenment.

Earth people are now on the way to becoming equal to the Star people! Earth, as a whole, is on its way to becoming an active and responsible member in the corridors of our particular Galactic Federation.

Every Seeker of Enlightenment has to read this great work—*S.T.A.R. Philosophy*.

All the Worldwide Masters of Pyramid Spiritual Societies Movement are conveying their sincere appreciation.

Brahmarshi Patriji

Founder, Pyramid Spiritual Societies Movement

Preface to the Third Edition

This book was originally published by CoRecreational Media Group in March 2013. During its first year in print, sales skyrocketed as its ideas profoundly touched the lives of readers not only across the United States and Canada but also in the Netherlands, France, and India. Absorbing the book's guidance, they began to journey into the etheric realm and discover their sacred states of being, emerging with insights into their own perfection. These they used to manage everyday challenges and unforeseen obstacles. Simultaneously requests started pouring in for a companion volume.

In October 2014, I took S.T.A.R. philosophy to Singapore and to India, where I addressed a gathering of more than two thousand members of the Pyramid Spiritual Societies Movement. Brahmarshi Patriji, the movement's founder, contributed a foreword to the second edition of *S.T.A.R. Philosophy*. Soon thereafter, book 2 in the S.T.A.R. series, now titled *The Fascinated Observer,* which I coauthored with Kristy Sweetland, was released.

As more and more readers came to see creation through the eyes of a creator, the philosophy took root. There were dreams of new alliances, such as S.T.A.R.-based mediation, S.T.A.R.-based playgrounds, S.T.A.R.-based oncology, and S.T.A.R.-based parenting. Already one of my dreams has come to fruition: as the corporate secretary for Pristina, Inc., a young company located in Santa Fe, New Mexico, I have observed the principles of S.T.A.R. guiding the company into new ways of doing business—no force, only synchronicity. In the fall of 2016, Life University in Telangana, India, asked to add the S.T.A.R. series to its curriculum.

This third edition of *S.T.A.R. Philosophy* is to be published in March 2017 under the imprint of Cauda Pavonis. My desire is that it will serve as a magic wand for the divine nature of all humans seeking new ways of being on earth.

CONTEMPLATION

Be the Love

(to be spoken aloud for vibrational attunement)

Individually and collectively,
I am enveloped in the love of the divine Creator.

I express gratitude and appreciation.

I hold the intention to focus the totality that I am,
bringing all aspects into crystalline clear alignment.

I hold the intention that by means of the conscious
attunement of the totality that I am,
that I may experience
THE FULLNESS OF THE OCTAVES OF LIGHT
that are ever present.

I now hold in my sacred heart the intention and
awareness to align with
THE FULL OCTAVE OF MY ORIGINAL GOD TONE,
which already exists in all that is within and around me.

I now hold in my sacred heart the intention and
awareness to align with
THE FULL OCTAVE TONE OF KINDNESS,
which already exists in all that is within and around me.

I now hold in my sacred heart the intention and
awareness to align with
THE FULL OCTAVE TONE OF WISDOM,
which already exists in all that is within and around me.

I now hold in my sacred heart the intention and
awareness to align with
THE FULL OCTAVE TONE OF PLAY,
which already exists in all that is within and around me.

I now hold in my sacred heart the intention and
awareness to align with
THE FULL OCTAVE TONE OF IMAGINATION,
which already exists in all that is within and around me.

I now hold in my sacred heart the intention and
awareness to align with
THE FULL OCTAVE TONE OF DIVINE HUMAN SERVICE,
which already exists in all that is within and around me.

I now hold in my sacred heart the intention and
awareness to align with
THE FULL OCTAVE TONE OF SPIRITUAL STRENGTH,
which already exists in all that is within and around me.

I now hold in my sacred heart the intention and awareness to align with
THE FULL OCTAVE TONE OF JOY,
which already exists in all that is within and around me.

I now hold in my sacred heart the intention and awareness to align with
THE FULL OCTAVE TONE OF COLLABORATION,
which already exists in all that is within and around me.

I now hold in my sacred heart the intention and awareness to align with
THE FULL OCTAVE TONE OF NOW.

The qualities of love of the divine Creator have permeated the totality that I am at a full octave, I now hold the intention that I "Be" this love.

In being the love of the divine Creator, I hold the intention that by means of this love,

I become the instrument of
THE GOLDEN AGE OF DIVINE LOVE.

I am both the seed and the fruit of the new earth.

I deliberately create divine good.
AND SO IT IS.

(After reading this meditation aloud, go into an internal space for silent integration before continuing.)

Definition of Words
within the Term S.T.A.R.

S.T.A.R.: When one aligns with the will
and love of the divine Creator
SURRENDER to the tranquility of
knowing human divinity
TRUST in wholeness to express
ALLOW human divinity to evolve
RECEIVE with appreciation and gratitude

THE ESSENTIAL QUALITIES OF THE
S.T.A.R. PHILOSOPHY

WHOLENESS (human divinity)

SELF-LOVE

PLAY (the now moment)

EMBODIMENT OF THE EXPANDED GOLDEN RULE

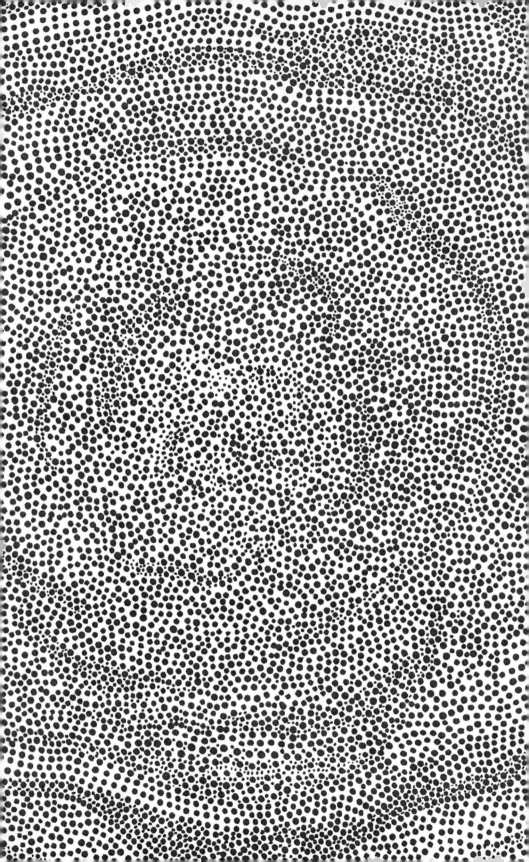

Who Am I?

Since the dawn of humanity, answering this question has been our individual and collective quest. We go on a quest complete with a multitude of experiences on planet earth and from those quests and experiences we create our identity.

If we come to believe we are only the human Jane or Joe personality and that all else is separate from our being, we will learn to use force to create or control our world.

If we can know ourselves as truly divine humans, we can use *imagination* to create interesting new ways to experience the experience NOW and in the future.

Who Are the Others?

They are you. You are them. We are ALL the One Consciousness. The person passing you on the street is part of you. Separation is the illusion, and although we are all unique, Unity is the truth.

Does this understanding not shift your love for "them?"

In the quantum field (the field of discrete units of energy), they are you and you are them and we are beyond time, personality and environment. We are just "being" as a part of a greater I Am, the All That Is where infinite possibilities are available from which to create what we experience on earth.

Imagine that You Are a Divine Human

Imagine that it is possible to be a divine human—to actually BE the love of the divine Creator fully at one with all of creation. Put aside your doubts. Unplug from anything that led you to believe that you are anything less than divine. Move in wholeness into that moment and choose to stay there if you wish. You have been gifted with free will, so at any moment you can move back into the comfort of old beliefs or you can stay awhile and play, merging with the will of your very own divine nature.

IMAGINATION HELPS US TO MERGE WITH OUR DIVINE NATURE.

When we merge with our divine nature our dream might be:

With the S. T.A.R. philosophy, I can explore the idea that the enlightened figures, such as Jesus, attempted to assist humanity in owning: It is our birthright to know ourselves as divine humans. Being intuitive, I innately feel that message to be true. I am the divine Creator in human form. However after eons of being told by authority figures that humans must look outside of themselves for "God," knowing or owning our divinity has become challenging. So, even if it is difficult for me to own my divinity, I will do my best to stay open to the possibility.

I know that being the divine Creator in human form, I am, therefore, also a creator being. I hold a frequency and what I emit from that frequency creates the structure of my personal experiences. The resonant frequency that I am willing to receive is in complete harmonic resonance with the frequency I am creating. Thus, with the willingness to expand my frequency to that of the divine Creator, I am fully capable of creating the new experiences and embodying what I have come to know as the Golden Age of Divine Love.

WHAT ARE THE NEW THINGS I AM HERE TO CREATE?

Before the creation can become manifest, first a new foundation is required to support our blooming into the Golden Age of Divine Love. I imagine that all I am about to create and experience comes from that new foundation of knowing and owning, that I am All That Is. I feel that knowing. I have free will and can stay or stop playing anytime. While reading this book I am merely entering into a place where I can imagine that this owning of my divinity is possible.

To get into a state of being where I can begin to imagine new possibilities, I choose to do a quick visualization exercise.

FOUR PILLARS VISUALIZATION

First, I imagine that I can see four foundational pillars. These pillars serve as *anchors*. Their purpose is to anchor me firmly in the new paradigm of knowing that I am All That Is.

I require that each pillar be fully secure to avoid imbalances.

I imagine that the first pillar represents the full expression, acceptance and declaration of my human divinity. I accept and hold onto the first pillar until I feel at one with it.

The second pillar represents the full expression, acceptance and declaration of self-love. I accept and hold onto the second pillar until I feel at one with it.

The third pillar represents living in the NOW moment (the definition of play). I accept and hold onto the third pillar until I feel at one with it.

The fourth pillar represents living the Expanded Golden Rule—"Do unto all creation as I would have all of creation do unto me." I accept and hold onto the fourth pillar until I feel at one with it.

Once I am firmly planted on this foundation, I imagine myself coming together with others in community knowing my wholeness while respecting their human divinity, their energy field, their boundaries and their space.

With my new foundation and four pillars, I know I have a method to support myself in shifting to the now to express my experiences. These effect the awareness of others within my community and they can move forward to share it with their communities. These gentle actions create expanded states of being in people who can then choose to move onward to touch others. All this combines to allow the new earth expression to flower.

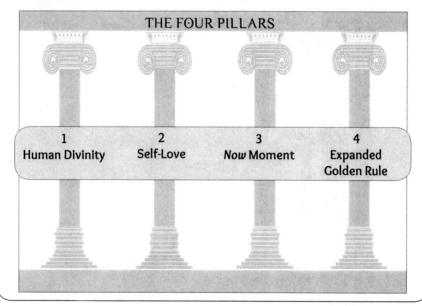

THE FOUR PILLARS

1	2	3	4
Human Divinity	Self-Love	*Now* Moment	Expanded Golden Rule

DREAM, IMAGINE AND BE

Thank you for imagining that you are a divine human and for considering accepting a new foundation on which to express your experiences. Could it be that collectively, knowing ourselves as divine humans, we are on planet earth to create, anchor, nourish and grow the new ways of being on earth, the Golden Age of Divine Love? I believe this as truth. I believe this is why I am on planet earth now and why you have found this book.

NOW, LET US CONTINUE TO PLAY AND DISCOVER HOW WE WOULD DREAM AND IMAGINE NEW WAYS OF BEING ON EARTH.

THE INNER WORKINGS OF THE
S.T.A.R. PHILOSOPHY

My Inner Compass

The first time I heard the acronym S.T.A.R. expressed in this way was from James F. Jereb, PhD. In 2007, I visited with James at Stardreaming (stardreaming.org), the sacred site he had been instructed to build by his "inner voices." At the time, S.T.A.R. to me was only an acronym. The power of the words that S.T.A.R. represented had not penetrated my awareness.

One morning, not long after meeting James, I went out on my porch with the word "surrender" circling in my mind. Definition of the word "surrender" was linked to an instant association with history—specifically Napoleon surrendering at Waterloo. That association was easy to retrieve, but I was seeking something more expansive that I imagined would help me discover the secret for living in heaven on earth. My mind wandered off from Waterloo to focus on the concept of particles of creation. It had occurred to me that the particles were being expressed as those dots in many of James' paintings. The space in-between the dots made me think of infinity or infinity space, which I knew was not out there, beyond my physical body, but in me as well. I knew that I was and am connected to All That Is by means of infinity space.

"Infinity is the unlimited potential of God, which first manifested as awareness, then as love, next as spirit, and finally as an infinite supply of adamantine particles that can be arranged with endless possibilities. Now remember that as an aspect of God, you are part of infinity, not part of the resulting structure."[1]

---

1.   Glenda Green, *Love Without End: Jesus Speaks* (Sedona, AZ: Spiritis Publishing, 1999), p. 176.

That morning, the "Ah-ha!" moment appeared when all of my thoughts came smoothly together: I am to surrender my intention to the space of infinity, in-between the dots or particles of creation and place it there with appreciation and gratitude, then trust and allow. That was it! My power would not be taken away, as had happened with Napoleon. On the contrary, I would actually become divinely powerful. I would be imagining and choosing my experiences as a divine human rather than surrendering as a powerless human. My intention could grow in the space of infinity, which I now refer to as the quantum field, by means of the expansive emotional energy of appreciation and gratitude. Surrender could then become a way of being from which I would express my divine will.

Since that moment, exploring the meaning of S.T.A.R. has been at the front of my mind, for I feel intuitively that it represents an irrefutable law of creation. Mastery is a process, and even now as I write this book, the magnitude of the S.T.A.R. philosophy is continually expanding. For me, S.T.A.R. is a gift for humanity, given to assist us in manifesting the way to create heaven on earth and live into the Golden Age of Divine Love.

SIMPLE BUT NOT EASY

At first glance, many people may believe that applying S.T.A.R. to their lives is simple. To be given a formula for success is simple. Knowing or memorizing is the easy part. To understand, integrate and live the energy of the formula is the challenge. When we begin the assimilation process and add new ideas, the brain and the heart must start to form a coherent (aligned) wave of possibility (the energy of thoughts) for the next S.T.A.R. action/choice to occur. This is choosing and acting as a divine human.

Another factor which may block us from accessing S.T.A.R. is the chemical dependency of the body on old patterned subconscious thoughts and actions, which has been masterfully explained by Dr. Joe Dispenza in his book, *Breaking the Habit of Being Yourself: How to Lose Your Mind and Create a New One.* These old habits can block the new thoughts and actions of the emerging divine human.

The constant exchange and monitoring between the brain and the body begins to shift from feeling the way we think to thinking the way we feel, and a habit is created. The body has memorized the feeling and is producing chemicals creating an addiction to the feeling. For example, we experience a situation that causes us to suffer. We then remember the situation, which causes the identical chemicals of suffering to be produced.

HOW THE BODY & MIND CREATE HABITS

THINKING THE WAY WE FEEL

monitor and exchange information

BODY memorizes

positive and negative feelings

BRAIN produces chemicals that are transmitted to BODY creating an imprint or addiction

BODY memorizes both chemicals and feelings originating in the BRAIN

=

HABIT CREATED

FEELING THE WAY WE THINK

When I immediately associated "surrender" with Waterloo and a terrible outcome, I blocked myself from getting to a different perspective on "surrender." The more I thought about this "terrible" situation, the more my body remembered that feeling, and it began to create a subconscious craving for the "suffering chemicals." It then sent messages to the brain which continued this pattern. To merely think that I will not focus on suffering is not sufficient since as shared in *Breaking the Habit of Being Yourself*, 95% of the mind is producing subconscious automatic programs, which override my new thought or intention.

One way to effect a change in thought, intention or action consciously and to override the subconscious programming is to dream or imagine in the present moment. In that now moment, emotions generated from thoughts of the past or future do not exist, which allow the mind to shift. This shift away from fear, suffering or low self-esteem creates a new chemical relationship with the body. Changes in thoughts, feelings, emotional reactions and behaviors send new signals to the body. We can break the negative chemical habit by being consciously aware and knowing that we can condition our system to positive emotions. New frequency thoughts, when producing positive feelings, result in feeling the way we think instead of thinking the way we feel.

> In the *now* moment, emotions generated from thoughts of the past or future do not exist.

S.T.A.R. is simple to describe, but I found that it was not so easy to integrate without doing "inner alchemy" work. I needed to break my chemical dependency on past emotions in order to create the brain circuits that would allow me to move into a different thought paradigm. The specific work, conducted in lucid dream state, focused on a review of the wounds of the past to identify the origin of the emotions caused by fear and rejection. On one occasion in contemplation, the image of my mother appeared. I saw her detached emotionally and critical of my youthful behavior and spoken words. I remembered that this pattern was apparent throughout my childhood. Each episode that I brought forth was of not receiving love and validation, so in order to create new brain circuits I chose to shift the memory to an image of my mother holding me in her arms.

The love circuit between my heart and the heart of my mother felt palpable. The affection that I had felt was missing in the memories of my past began to pour into my heart. New memories of my relationship with my mother were created. I believe that the habitual feeling of rejection that had fed me emotionally for all of my adult life was changed, and that by choice I replaced it with a feeling of acceptance and love. These new memories will change my future, which will no longer be tainted by past negative emotions. I will move into that future with the recorded image of me lovingly embraced by my mother on all occasions in the past, present and future. I am choosing to chemically feel the way I think. When we change the way we perceive the past, we create a change in the quantum field, which creates new outcomes for us even when we find our self in similar situations. The point is that our field is different, therefore, our future self MUST adapt in new ways.

The inner alchemy work of conscious choice is simple but not easy. We have to clear and release that which we do not wish to repeat so that even subconsciously we choose to create our reality exonerated from our most habitual patterns.

So you may look at the acronym S.T.A.R. and think, "That is simple. I can do it." And yes, you CAN do it. However, before you start playing with this philosophy, let's look more deeply into the definition of each aspect of S.T.A.R.

SURRENDER TO THE TRANQUILITY OF KNOWING ONE'S HUMAN DIVINITY

You may wonder who is surrendering to what? Our human personality is surrendering to the tranquility that comes from owning our human divinity (wholeness). Knowing our human divinity, we can surrender to what is relevant to us in the moment. We can release the pain of the past and the fear of the future. Release control and surrender to the present moment. True surrender is the surrender of our will to that of the divine will. The personality identification with individual existence, or the ego, believes itself to be independent of the One Consciousness and makes choices based on its perceived need for survival. Suffering and fear exist in the personality. Choices are made out of alignment with the innate wisdom within the heart. Surrendering the personality to the innate wisdom of the heart, or one's human divinity, allows for suffering and fear to lose their power. Survival is no longer the driving force when the personality surrenders to the infinite oneness of All That Is and our state of being transforms into a state of contentment or tranquility.

You may wonder, how does one know if they are truly a divine human? Go within and ask for the grace of the divine Creator to reveal that belief, that knowing—no longer seek this wisdom or validation from outside of oneself. Ask to become fully aware of the One Consciousness which expresses, experiences and feels through the consciousness of the human vessel.

Yes, I, Nina the author, am divine. I always have been. I always will be. I am NOT extraordinary. You too are divine. The truth is, even though we may doubt it, we are ALL divine. When we surrender to knowing we ARE divine, we move into a state of grace.

Living in the now moment as a divine human is a new aspect to add to our growing understanding of surrender. To surrender sounds so disempowering to the personality. Our personality, not our divinity, has attachments to memories of a traditional way of thinking about surrender, such as when Napoleon surrendered power, glory, prestige, wealth and pride, all that defined his self-worth, to Wellington at Waterloo. That little self, the personality, will fight hard to not let any semblance of that happen to us. We may have spent a lifetime striving to be in control of our external environment; this is why our personality will not feel comfortable surrendering if it involves loss. The personality believes that achieving material possessions and acclaim is the measure of success and a tool for survival.

The surrender in S.T.A.R. is not about loss or survival. On the contrary, it is about power.

The power behind surrendering to our divine human is that we begin to make conscious choices in alignment with the will of the divine Creator, and thus the flow and synchronicity in our lives accelerate. These conscious choices made in the now have no bias attached to them that was created by any memory of past suffering or fear of the future. They are crystalline thoughts inspired from our innate knowing. Control is not necessary because the aligned will of the divine Creator wishes only our highest good.

Now, in the *now*, is the time/no time to surrender. Let go of force and let in the magic that can occur from attraction and magnetism. We can remove all attachment to emotional patterns and achieve a state of being where everything we observe and experience "just is." Shifting the measurement of self-worth from personal achievements and possession to a belief that our true self-worth comes from knowing our human divinity is a major factor. Our self-worth is communicated to others as an inner light which emanates with the frequency of love and draws people and circumstances to us.

As creators confidently aware of our connection to Source, we can most efficiently create by surrendering our intentions, dreams and visions. We let go of them. We allow the space to open up for the extraordinary to exist. We place the thought energy, emanating from our heart, into the multi-dimensional field. Then we trust, allow and receive.

Quantum physics describes what occurs in the field when this dynamic is fully engaged.

1. The thought is energy expressed as a wave of possibility until it is collapsed into particle form by means of conscious observation.

2. Our personality wants to cause a premature collapse based on old conditioning and patterns, which makes the creation of new experiences difficult or impossible.

3. If we surrender our will to the will of the One Consciousness and allow our human divinity to collapse the waves of possibility, then our intention is expanded and expressed in new and inspiring ways, and we are provided unimaginable opportunities for growth on our spiral of life.

The surrender in S.T.A.R. is like a child surrendering to the will of the mother. We are surrendering to what Eckhart Tolle describes as "a field of pure potentiality rather than something that is already defined."[2] By doing so, we allow the next "most perfect experience" to manifest for

---

2. Eckhart Tolle, *The New Earth: Awakening to Your Life's Purpose* (New York, NY: Penguin Group, 2005), p. 109.

the journey we are each taking towards the full awareness of our divinity. The experience will be perfect no matter what it looks like—because we created it. Surrendering to our wholeness does not guarantee a smooth journey. We don't change directions or give up patterns of behavior easily. It is often discomfort which is the catalyst to change moving us in a new direction or expanded experience.

LIVING IN SURRENDER (AN EVERYDAY LIFE EXAMPLE)

What does this definition of surrender look like when lived? Is it possible to experience surrender, as a divine human, while sitting in the Chicago airport waiting and waiting as the departure time for the plane keeps getting delayed? My recent experience feels like a perfect example of the power of surrender, so I'll share what happened to me.

Barbara, my friend of several years, had invited me to join her at a gathering she was hosting at her home on Crane's Pond in Richland, Michigan. My home is in Santa Fe, New Mexico, an hour and a half away from the Albuquerque International Sunport Airport. Arriving in Grand Rapids mid-afternoon was my goal, since I had an hour drive from the terminal to Barbara's house. In order to achieve the desired arrival time, I had to get up at 3:00 a.m. for a 6:00 a.m. flight out of Albuquerque. To fly north, I had to fly south to Phoenix and catch a plane there to Chicago, where another plane would fly me to Grand Rapids to arrive at 4:05 p.m. The day would be long, but by flying on a Thursday, I would have all of Friday sitting by the pond visiting with Barbara to recover before the anticipated Saturday gathering.

All the early connections went perfectly, and I arrived in Chicago with a little over an hour to change terminals, get some lunch and arrive at my gate for a 2:15 p.m. departure. The saga began when I was told that the terminal bus was not running and that it would be best if I walked...and walked to terminal A. The exercise actually felt good after being stationary for so long. When I arrived at gate A3, it felt as if something was wrong because a plane to Montreal was posted, not my plane to Grand Rapids.

The attendant told me that I was in the correct location. My plane would take off at 2:50 p.m. I called Barbara, whose phone was on silent mode, to tell her in case she had not left the house. She called me back from the grocery store saying that she and her husband had already left the house and would just go on to the Grand Rapids airport and wait.

As I was reading my book, a voice came on over the loudspeaker saying that there was a gate change for the flight to Grand Rapids and to please go to gate A8 for a 5:00 p.m. departure. I got up and went to the screen to double check that I had heard the new information correctly. Sure enough, it said Grand Rapids, gate A8, departure at 5:00 p.m. Fortunately, my book was very engaging. At 4:40 p.m. I looked at my ticket and saw that it did not have a group assignment, so I approached the attendant early. As he was swiping the ticket across the electronic reader, the machine did not respond. The attendant looked at my ticket and said that I was at the wrong gate trying to board the wrong plane. I had to go to gate A2.

Oh my gosh, had I missed my plane? How come there were two planes going to the little airport in Grand Rapids? I ran to gate A2, since my plane's departure gate had been changed. While breathing fast, I located the screen. My plane had not left, but it was posted with a delayed departure of 6:10 p.m. I was so relieved to have not missed my connection that I barely absorbed the fact that now I had to wait until 6:10 p.m. to fly out of Chicago. Fortunately, the battery in my cell phone was well-charged because just after I had notified Barbara, I had to call her again to say that the plane was delayed one more time and would now arrive at 7:45 p.m.

My book came to an end, and I began to notice fatigue setting in. The people around me were stirring. When I looked up, I noticed that gate A3, my original departure gate, also had a posting for a flight to Grand Rapids. A line was forming to sign up for standby on this flight, which was scheduled to leave at 6:32 p.m. I gathered my carry-on bag and joined the line at the counter for my first standby experience.

While the line was slowly getting shorter, a passenger began yelling at one of the attendants, "Why didn't you tell me when I approached you? Now I am out of line and..."

When it was my turn to sign up for one of the rare standby positions, I asked the attendant if it was worthwhile to do so. I was told that it would be fine to add my name to the list that would soon include several more names. When I returned to my seat, I noticed the electronic screen at gate A3 had posted the standby names. The first two names were checked and my unchecked name was number eight on the list. This did not seem very encouraging.

I called Barbara and asked if she could identify a hotel for me to spend the night, when I would finally arrive in Grand Rapids, so that she could go home. As we were talking, the gate A3 Grand Rapids plane was being boarded. I asked Barbara not to drive home immediately since I was posted on standby on a different plane. When she hung up, I felt discouraged as I contemplated a long night in the Chicago airport. My conscious awareness went deep inside me, and I surrendered. I let go of all events surrounding me. I realized there was nothing I had control over. I then heard my internal voice say, "Please just take care of me."

I looked up at the screen and my name was still not checked, but it was magically in position four. By now all the passengers were on the plane. Then over the loud speaker I heard, "Last call for Nina Brown." I leaped out of the chair and ran to the attendant who handed me a ticket. I fumbled with my cell phone as I walked down the plank toward the plane. Barbara's number was misdialed twice in my excitement. When I got to my front row, aisle seat I calmed down enough to dial correctly, "Barbara, I am on the plane!"

I had intuitively surrendered to the knowing that Eckhart Tolle has masterfully expressed. My external reality is a reflection of my state of consciousness and less a result of my actions. No amount of action will effect a change in my exterior reality unless I shift my conscious awareness. Without this shift, modified versions of the same world I have known will continue.

When we choose to surrender our personality to our human divinity, we are imagining a gentler way of experiencing our life. We are trusting that the alignment of our will with that of the divine Creator will attract the perfect experience for our journey on the spiral of life.

SURRENDER TO THE TRANQUILITY OF KNOWING HUMAN DIVINITY.

TRUST IN WHOLENESS TO EXPRESS

You might wonder who is trusting what? Our personality is trusting that we are sovereign beings fully capable of authoring and being responsible for the flow of our experience on earth. The personality self has been in charge for so long that the thought of letting go is terrifying. That personality is the identity that other people associate with us. I am Nina the mother, the student, the teacher, the author. Those are just a few of the personalities or roles I play in life. Though important, they are not the core of who I am—my core is my divinity. It existed before I came into this physical body and it will exist after I leave it behind.

When our personality is threatened, we instantly associate the feeling of fear with survival. We believe we will lose control. Trust of self, others or the world becomes non-existent. "Impossible," says the personality, which is why we have to move out of time, environment and body into an octave that we can completely trust our human divinity. Within a state of alpha brain wave patterning, during meditation or in lucid dream state, we can move our conscious awareness into the now and relax in this safe space trusting that our dreams, visions and new choices will be expressed by means of our alignment with the One Consciousness.

One example of "letting-go" trust is the trust we have in the physician who prescribes our medication. We go to doctors with whom we feel comfortable, so much so that we place the well-being of our bodies in their ability to choose a specific drug accurately. We are not students of pharmacology so we trust that specialty is the physician's expertise. The "T" in S.T.A.R. represents a trust of that magnitude, but in the now we are trusting the wisdom that comes from our innate knowing (not in choosing drugs but in making life choices). Let me tell you Carol's story to illustrate.

FLOWING INTO TRUST (TWO UNIQUE LIFE EXAMPLES)

Carol and I had lunch together one day as members of a weekly business networking group. There were just the two of us at the table since the other two members, we learned half way through the meal, were sitting a few tables over wondering where we were. Because of the intimacy of our situation, we were able to move beyond business to my favorite topic, human divinity. Carol seemed fine with this new direction for our lunch conversation.

I shared with my new acquaintance that I was working on a second book and was exploring expansive definitions of four words: surrender, trust, allow and receive. Something I must have said triggered a comment from Carol: "People are being sedated too much. We are sitting back and allowing this to happen." She shared that her son had recently left the nest for college and that, as she was adjusting daily to this new situation, she was simultaneously experiencing the onset of menopause. Carol told me that she found herself so out of balance that she went to see her personal physician who asked if Carol would consider taking an anti-depressant drug.

TRUST and listen to what your conscious awareness is communicating to you.

Carol felt uncomfortable with the suggestion. She decided that she wanted to experience these two life-changing events fully and to not mask the feelings. It felt to her that when she had worked through the depression and found a new course for her life that she would possibly have learned from the experience. Carol listened to what her conscious awareness was communicating to her, and she trusted the message so much that she chose to not accept the suggestion of an authority figure. (Carol's decision was the perfect choice for her. This story of trusting inner wisdom is chosen only to represent one person's journey.)

There was a time in my own journey that I strongly felt my body pulling me into a cycle of negative or debilitating emotions. That cycle continued until I figured out how to put a stop to that emotional charge and to trust the flow of events for which I knew I was a co-creator with Source.

The background to my story began when I again attended the weekly networking lunch in Santa Fe, which I attend with the intention to meet interesting people. On this occasion, I met Franz, who presented himself as a business consultant. By the time our extended lunch hour came to an end, I understood that Franz represented European investors who were looking for green, sustainable opportunities in the United States. My intuition kicked in and memories of when I had been involved years ago in the venture capital industry raced into my mind. Who did I know who might be a good connection? Ah, Andy was the one. He lives in California and is surrounded by cutting-edge thinkers. I would give him a call.

Andy was delighted that I had asked, and he quickly recommended that I contact his good friend Ray, who lives in Oregon. For years Andy, Ray and others have been concentrating on the development of a new industry, biochar, that uses a process called pyrolysis to turn organic waste into a carbon-rich soil augmentation. As an industry, biochar is currently fragmented and not being expressed at its full capacity. Ray felt strongly that with a major investment he could coordinate research, education, manufacturing and product to unify biochar's growth as a soil enhancement and cost-effective water treatment procedure. That sounded very good to me. I thought, "Perhaps by means of my introduction of investor to entrepreneur, I would be a catalyst for planetary cleansing! I'll do it!"

I searched my memory for the correct procedure for being a "Finder," the steps that one goes through before making the introduction. The details were a little rusty, but I put one foot in front of the other. First there was to be a contract between me and Ray called a Finder's Fee Agreement. Since I belong to a small business consulting group, I ran the details by their experts. I learned that the federal government wanted to know what I was up to. The experts informed me that I was required to be a broker/dealer to undertake this introduction. Well, the broker/dealer document was fourteen pages long and filled with legal, government language—ugh!

> As you access new octaves of TRUST you begin to learn to discern where, when and with whom to place your trust.

This was the tipping point. I chose not to put my trust in the government on this occasion, but into the multi-dimensional field of infinite possibility. The email that I wrote to Ray said that the introduction would be made and if he would choose to show appreciation in the form of a donation, that I would be pleased to receive it. I was declaring to the universe that I was sending out energy and that my expectation was that it would be returned in kind in a magical, yet unknown manner.

Once I made this unconventional choice, I felt that all would flow with ease and grace, but there was to be even more trusting as the days unfolded. Ray and I were to meet in Ashland on Monday, September 24th with the possibility of others showing up to meet me. I planned my trip through northern California with time to stop and visit the redwoods. That choice was restorative for me. On fall equinox, I climbed Mt. Shasta with friends and intentionally left my cell phone behind to experience the magic of the mountain undisturbed. When it was turned back on there were SO many phone calls from Ray saying, "Where are you? We are waiting! Someone drove down from Portland to meet you (over 300 miles). I am not looking good. Can you call so we can save this meeting?" All of these calls were made on Sunday while I was on Mt. Shasta in Panther Meadow meditating. Ray had the wrong day for our meeting!

I called Ray as soon as the clock struck nine in the morning. The voice on the other end of the phone had no energy. It was very difficult for me to speak with such lifeless feedback. The email that I had sent immediately after hearing the messages had not been read, so I had to start from the beginning. I had new information to add to the fact that we both were off by one day in our plans to meet. My host had recently shared with me that he is a consultant in environmental remediation and that he works on cleaning the water that goes into the San Francisco Bay. That contact seemed like a possible match for the biochar industry.

I walked from my host's porch overlooking Mt. Shasta into the den and gave the phone to him so that he could speak directly to Ray. I watched as his head went up and down and he made brief comments like, "I am intrigued. I would like to see a demonstration." After I hung up with Ray, the statement, "Perhaps we can do a pilot project with biochar," was shared with me. Wow, the universe had presented a potential investor, a green product needing capital for expansion and now a potential study and client. I, however, still felt my stomach churning from the emotions caused by learning of the missed meeting.

After leaving my friends in Mt. Shasta, I drove to Ashland, where my scheduled meeting with Ray was to have taken place. I could not stop my mind from going over and over the details of the missed meeting. Every time there was a mile marker, the sign said, "Portland 332 miles" or "Portland 300 miles." I could feel negative emotions swirling around my body when I thought of the annoyed individual who drove down from Portland to meet me. Nothing I thought or told myself could stop the reliving of this awful experience. It was wearing me down. Then I remembered a lecture given by Amit Goswami, PhD, describing his style of meditation. He suggested that we move the energy from the head to the heart and expand it out into the multi-dimensional field. So I tried it. Every time I thought of disappointing Ray, I quickly moved the energy to my heart, which began to open wider and wider. Using the metaphor of computer software, it was like click and drag, click and drag, click and drag until my brain circuits began to refire and rewire to the new way of being.

My thoughts shifted, and I began to trust that the universe was creating through me. Why had these events rearranged themselves? I had done nothing wrong. I knew that, "Everything just was." When I arrived in Ashland, there was an email from Andy which encouraged me to meet with Ray, so I called. Sure enough, Ray's voice was different and the energy exchange was elevated. He said he would like very much to meet me.

When we were having a wonderful dinner at Larks, the restaurant in the Ashland Springs Hotel, Ray told me that his friend from Portland had been told that the meeting might not happen. He had chosen to come anyway. Apparently, a team had gathered and gone over the many details of their biochar vision, which was exactly the next step required by the potential investor, the creation of a business plan. As Ray was speaking, I understood that my presence would have diverted that focus, and that where I belonged was right there having a long, intimate sharing with the original visionary, so that he would have more confidence in me and me in him.

What I had innately known, but which was now confirmed, was that Ray understood the flow of the universe. He completely "got" why I had chosen not to present him with a binding contract. He completely "got" why his meetings were for two days, each day being unique and perfect. When I shared with him how I turned the internal chemistry in my body around from negative emotions to positive emotions, he immediately said, "Write that down. Write down how you became comfortable with uncertainty."

Having studied Eckhart Tolle, I wrote, "I am able to live with uncertainty and I can enjoy it. When I become comfortable with uncertainty, infinite possibilities are able to open up in my life."

What I observed with this experience was that my discomfort had came from my wishing to control events, and that when I let go and trusted the flow, an inner peace came over me. As life unfolded, I was then able to see why I had created a different yet perfect outcome. I am to remember to allow the leap, the quantum leap.

> I had seen no path from here to there,
> yet it appeared.
> We need merely trust, and it is so.
> We are that powerful.
> Let us live every *now* moment in
> alignment with the One Consciousness.

TRUST, LET GO AND FLOW

If we know ourselves as divine, the play begins and we live in the *now* moment. Let go! Life then begins to flow with ease and grace. This is our birthright. Trust that wholeness will catch us as we imagine jumping off the cliff of illusionary security and comfort. We can do this with the innate knowing that comes from deep within our sacred heart.

Then as we do, so too will others. We become the model for others to realize that they too are divine humans, and they too can play in the now moment. This is the new earth. This is the Golden Age of Divine Love when we trust in our human divinity to guide us on our journey on the spiral of life.

TRUST IN WHOLENESS TO EXPRESS.

ALLOW HUMAN DIVINITY TO EVOLVE

You may wonder, who is to allow what? Wholeness is to allow what has been chosen to evolve. A divine human has no investment in outcome knowing that whatever transpires has the potential to move us one step further on the spiral of life. The issue, challenge or circumstance is neither good nor bad. It merely is, and it has the potential of causing delicious emotions and feelings.

"I allow the form of the moment, good or bad, to be as it is and so do not become a participant in human drama. To me there is only this moment, and this moment is as it is...Only if I resist what happens am I at the mercy of what happens, and the world will determine my happiness and unhappiness."[3]

Resistance is like Kryptonite in that it takes away all the power that comes when we allow. Resistance comes from the personality, which strives to control events to survive. Survival is necessary if one has a belief that consciousness is outside of matter and that there is a separation between the inner and outer reality. Quantum physics, however, has shown us that all matter is made up of energy, waves of possibility, and that the atom is not solid, as classical physics had suggested. So what does the personality think it is controlling? The answer is that it is attempting to control waves of possibility, which have collapsed into particle form by means of the One Consciousness expressing as you or me. There is just the illusion that the personality can have control and can resist. The illusion has been believed for so much of our lives that moving out of a state of resistance is more graceful when we apply the S.T.A.R. philosophy to what we are experiencing in that moment by means of conscious choice.

---

3. Ibid., p. 200.

Using Allow in the Worst Circumstances

Fortunately the S.T.A.R. philosophy was present in my life when the doors to our wellness center were forced to close in 2007. I could so easily have resisted the closing by making excuses or fighting back, but I chose to observe the flow with fascination and to dream of where it would take me next.

We (two other founders and myself) had put so much effort and energy into creating a vision for providing alternative medicine. The dream was enormous, and we had manifested most of what was needed for its expression. There were two clinics, one in Santa Fe and another in Albuquerque, New Mexico. We had attracted seed capital, a nurse to manage the neurosensory diagnostic equipment, an internal medicine physician and a team that was excited about the coordination between alternative and traditional modalities.

> I ALLOW.
> I choose to observe the flow with fascination and dream of where it might take me next.

My focus, in May of that year, was on answering numerous questions for our agent who was preparing our Medicare provider application. The process was horrific and totally outside my realm of experience, but I was determined to see its successful outcome. No independent insurance agent would cover our potentially lucrative treatment process, neurosensory diagnosis, without prior Medicare acceptance. The monthly diagnostic equipment rental was an on-going financial burden as we processed forms and answered questions for Medicare. Our expectation had been that the neurosensory diagnostic service, which we would provide in both clinics, would offer the most complete diagnostic evaluation available for dizziness, vertigo and imbalance. The complete array of non-invasive tests would allow our doctor to "see" the problem. These cutting edge tests also had the potential to provide abundant revenue for the clinics and would cover the expenses of the less profitable alternative modalities that were to be available.

In December, the financial stability of our vision was in trouble, as we continued to wait for an answer from Medicare. Then one early morning, I checked my email messages and found one from our agent. The clinics had been approved, but approval for the neurosensory diagnostic center was pending. We were informed that we had one month to have a certified audiologist on staff and then Medicare would grant approval. I typed into my computer's search engine, and the quest began. What I learned almost immediately was that to identify a certified audiologist in New Mexico would be very difficult. By three o'clock that same afternoon, however, a phone call came through from a perfect candidate who had an office in Santa Fe. He told me that our neurosensory equipment was a wonderful match for his professional vision, and that he would like to meet with us to discuss the possibility of working together. Miracle, our problem was solved, or so I thought.

The CEO, the president of our wellness clinics and I met with the audiologist, and we decided to draft an agreement explaining in detail our potential working relationship. At this point in my story, chaos set in and shifted my path. I got a call from the audiologist asking me why after two and a half weeks he had not received a draft of the expected agreement. Shock ran through me as he spoke those words. The details of why this occurred and why we missed the Medicare deadline are beyond the scope of this book. What is critical to the story is that I realized my life's path had to move in a different direction, and I allowed that to happen with no resistance. I felt every emotion intensely, but I had no resistance to the events that unfolded.

Feelings of every variety surged through me when we closed down the clinics and the diagnostic center. Fatigue was my strongest feeling. Mental and physical exhaustion filled my mind and my body. "Why?" was the predominant question, not "How could this be?" At this point in my life, I had been exposed to the philosophy of S.T.A.R., though I did not completely grasp its power

Thanks to Eckhart Tolle, I can say, *"One thing I do know: Life will give me whatever experience is most helpful for the evolution of my consciousness. How do I know this is the experience I need? Because this is the experience I am having at this moment."*[4]

BECOMING MORE FULLY AWARE OF THE HIDDEN BENEFITS

As I looked at every now moment going through this experience, I observed that with each day's passing, my self-worth was growing. The dissolution of the companies became my responsibility. The president had gone back to Texas and the CEO had a full-time job. I learned that even though I did not have a PhD, as was the case with the CEO and president, reading all the documents and untangling contracts was something that I was good at. I had given that power away during the creation process, even though I was fully aware that I was the principal person manifesting all that had appeared as we grew our vision. Upon completion of my work, it felt as if the dissolution papers, handed to me by the Public Regulations Commission, were the equivalent of me receiving an MBA, a master's degree in business administration.

Perhaps it was in less than two months that the universe opened the perfect door for me where I could create, not by force, but by using the

---

4. Ibid., p. 41. The quote has been paraphrased.

S.T.A.R. philosophy. James F. Jereb, the person from whom I had learned about S.T.A.R., invited me to assist in the maintenance, preservation and expansion of Stardreaming. "Miracles happen every day," says Forrest Gump's Mama.[5]

I allow the perfect doors and glorious miracles to be open to me.
I create, not by force, but through expansion.

A more global example of "allow" came to me while listening to Gregg Braden's audio book *The Isaiah Effect*. Braden speaks about traveling in the Himalayan Mountains visiting Tibetan monasteries. On one occasion, he described an opportunity that he had to speak with one of the monks about their prayers of compassion. He shared with the audience that had it not been for the fact that Tibetan refugees now live all over the world, since their displacement from their homeland by the Chinese government, we would not have knowledge of their formerly sequestered prayers of compassion. Braden asked if the monks prayed to be returned to their homeland. The answer was that their prayers were for compassion for all of creation. He then learned that the people have an expectation that Tibet will be returned to them. His conclusion in the audio book was that the Tibetans are in a state of allowing. As they wait and pray for compassion, the world is being enriched with the knowledge of that compassion as the Tibetan people move throughout the planet. They allow that at the perfect moment, when that work is complete,

---

5. *Forrest Gump*, Paramount Pictures, 1994.

Tibet will be returned to them. What one learns from this sharing is that allowing the One Consciousness to coordinate the absolute flow of life provides gifts to individuals and humanity of which our ego self can barely conceive.

The Tibetan people hold an intention and allow the details to Source. Their gift to the planet of the prayer of compassion has been a bridge to a more expansive state of being, but perhaps as we move into the Golden Age of Divine Love we no longer need a bridge. When we know deeply that we are one with all creation, then having compassion no longer serves us, for in doing so we create a state of separation between the other and the self. All that is now needed is love.

Dr. Joe Dispenza explains, "Hold a clear intention of what you want, but leave the 'how' details to the unpredictable quantum field. Let it orchestrate an event in your life in a way that is just right for you. If you're going to expect anything, expect the unexpected."[6]

Allowing can be easily confused with trust. In a way they do go hand in hand. But I would also invite you to consider that in order to allow, we first must trust that Source is providing the perfect outcome, and then we can allow that outcome to enter our experience.

ALLOW HUMAN DIVINITY TO EVOLVE.

---

6. Dr. Joe Dispenza, *Breaking the Habit of Being Yourself: How to Lose Your Mind and Create a New One* (Carlsbad, CA: Hay House, Inc., 2012), p. 25.

RECEIVE WITH APPRECIATION AND GRATITUDE

You may wonder how do we truly receive? Our wholeness is to receive the imagined and chosen potential with the passion of gratitude and appreciation, for what we desire already exists in the field of all possibilities.

Soon, as I make that statement, the next question is: *If that is true, why do my creations fail to manifest?* Visions and choices can easily be sabotaged by the dreamer, when we fail to listen to and follow the guidance that comes from within. Sometimes our guidance does not make logical sense simply because that guidance is beyond logic. When we succumb to the guidance of others, when it is not in alignment with our inner vibrational response, this blocks the natural flow of events. Lack of self-love also sabotages our creations.

When the waves of thought and feeling are coherent and aligned, they are much more powerful and pull us towards our desired reality.

~

Established patterns of being cause the body to automatically repel what it feels unworthy to receive. A lifetime of feeling shame or having a lack of self-worth establishes a chemical response in the body which subconsciously sends messages to the brain, "Feed me more of those deprecating thoughts!" The chemical exchange between the mind and the body can create an addiction that requires more and more to satisfy the ever increasing need of this habit.

According to Dr. Dispenza, no matter how much the mind might think that it wants to change a pattern, the internal cycle that has been created over time does not allow for a new expression of self without work. Going into no time/no space of the *now* in meditation allows for one to detach from the emotions of suffering of the past and fear of the future. In that space, new dreams can be created, which cause the

51

firing and wiring of the brain to change and new circuits to be created. Shame can be replaced by love for self. Unworthiness can be replaced with self-realization. When we have repeatedly imagined these new thoughts, we can receive without triggering old emotions that block the flow of the new and even the unimagined, which can fill us with emotions of love for self. We are worthy to receive all that is gifted, for we are divine humans and are to be honored by the universe for the work that we came to planet earth to do.

The feeling that I am not worthy has been with me a great deal of my life. If I am not worthy, how can I be worthy to receive? I rejected and did not internalize compliments that others gave me. I didn't feel good about myself, so I thought, why would anyone else see me differently? How could I, therefore, deserve to receive what it is that I imagine? It could never happen to me, perhaps to someone else, but not to me. We sabotage the flow in our lives with these limiting feelings. Until they are replaced, we will subconsciously continue to choose a limited expression of our dreams.

> Unworthiness can be replaced with self-realization.

LITTLE GIFT, BIG GIFT

I wish to share with you an example of how I could not internalize a compliment during the time in my life when I had low self-esteem. In the early 1990s, a friend suggested that I attend a self-help course offered by Landmark Education. At the end of the weekend, we were instructed to have someone tell us four things they liked about us and four things they did not like about us. I asked my friend to assist me with this assignment. What I observed after we were complete was that I had a clear memory of the words he spoke concerning my weaknesses, but no short-term memory of what he liked about me. I had been unable to integrate his expressed love for me.

Self-worth has come to me after a lot of inner alchemy work, which is a continuing process. One of the most effective times for me to do this work is early in the morning during lucid dream state, outside of time and space. Recently at just such a time, I moved my awareness into memories of my childhood to search for experiences I had where I thought and felt that I had not received. What came to me was when I was perhaps ten years old, Uncle Hobson, my father's youngest brother, came to visit us. He came bearing gifts for my older sister, Alix, and me. She received a large stuffed bear, and I was gifted a very much smaller, almost tiny, stuffed bear. This memory has popped in my mind a few times but I have never focused on its emotional influence on my body and what chemical response it has caused my body to memorize.

I was the younger sister, so it was natural that I would receive the smaller bear. I am sure that no one would consider giving the elder the smaller choice and the younger the larger choice. What came to me in this intense reflection was that this conditioning happened over and over during my life, creating a pattern of thinking and feeling less than. "Of course," my ego would say, "I should expect to receive less than. I am less than." That became my natural state of being. I understand now that my mind/body chemistry reinforced this feeling each time a "less than receiving" situation occurred or when I thought about a "less than receiving" situation. This was how I identify myself, and my body chemistry was masterfully reinforcing the condition that made me chemically comfortable.

As I delved deeper into this receiving mentality that the experience with the bears identified, the question occurred, "How do I change this behavior?" The answer came to me intuitively like an inner wisdom. I saw myself as a vortex that was spinning up as a giver. Then I called in a downward focused vortex changing the condition to one of receiving. I observed carefully and the former had not disappeared. The two were overlaid, putting me in a new environment of equally giving and receiving. What I had done was moved outside of my normal environment into a brand new one. As I write, I can sense being in the energy of this dynamic. I can see myself walking across the room in the center of these vortices. There is a knowing that I have changed my choice from being a giver to being both a giver and a receiver. A feeling of being worthy now allows me to receive the bounty from the quantum field. My dreams are now free to play in the multi-dimensional field of all possibility.

The most amazing "Ah-ha!" coming from my memory of the two bears is that today I am the owner of both. My sister, on entering the Carmelite monastery, relinquished all her possessions. She gave me her large stuffed brown bear. Both bears are now together in my home in Santa Fe, New Mexico. I had not taken the time to realize that while carrying the subconscious feeling of "less than," I was actually experiencing "more than" without realizing it. Fascinating.

As my feeling of self-worth has matured, my ability to manifest my intentions has increased as well. The original blocks or sabotaging emotions have diminished, allowing for the creative process to flow and for me to receive what it is I imagine or perhaps even more than I dream of.

EXPANSIVE OUTCOMES

It is fascinating to look back and see how an intended outcome can morph into something more expansive than I had been able to dream. This book that you are currently reading is just such an example. The story began in 2009 when I was called to write a book about who I am, where I come from and why I am on the planet. Being an author was so far out of my frame of reference, I said I would write the book, "Only in partnership with my divine self." Having said, "Yes," how was I to begin? Once again in my life, all that I needed began to appear. A friend suggested that I study from an individual who consults on book publishing. In lesson one, the teacher spoke about finding an agent who would represent me and my future book to publishers. Okay, I could do that. I found a free list on the internet and began sending several hundred letters out to agents around the country asking them if they would be interested in my book. "No." "No." "Thank you, no." I had a whole binder with query and rejection letters in alpha order. So, what was step two that the teacher was suggesting? I went through each step and slowly learned the art of self-publishing. That was not my intention, nor my choice and absolutely not my dream. I was committed at this point, so I just kept traveling down the path trusting and allowing what was presenting itself. One could have observed my process and made the deduction that I had not received what I had initially chosen: to be wanted as a new author by a publisher.

My first book, *Return of Love to Planet Earth: Memoir of a Reluctant Visionary*, was published in 2010, by my publishing company, Cauda Pavonis, and out it went into the world market. Sales occurred, and I was even encouraged to do a second more professional edition so that it could be better represented by my publicist who called it a "jewel." So perhaps I had the wrong initial intention because I had learned a lot about the fast-changing publishing business, and my book was well-received and actually won two awards in the category of New Age, Non-fiction, 2012.

My story is not over, because I have not shared with you how I have indeed received my original dream, but in a way that was more creative and magical. As my journey was unfolding, I met in 2012 another author while traveling in Egypt, Alison L. James, who was intrigued by my work, and who decided to write an article about it. She posted her writings on her site at Gather Insight and sent me a copy. "How lovely, thank you," was about all that I said. Then came the unexpected phone call from a stranger, Ja-lene Clark. We talked for a very long time, but I really wasn't sure why she was calling me, something about how she just knew that we needed to talk. I don't think she was sure why she was calling either. Then at the end of our conversation, Ja-lene told me that she would be coming to an event that I was producing in Santa Fe, the S.T.A.R. clinic. She asked if we could meet for lunch the day after the event to talk. That sounded like fun. Oh, and could I please send a copy of my book to her to read on the airplane.

Ja-lene had a major family event that easily could have kept her from coming to Santa Fe, but she came anyway. She attended our first S.T.A.R. clinic and, as we had planned, she was sitting on the porch of the Bishop's Lodge Ranch Resort and Spa at noon on Monday waiting for me. We had no time to speak during the weekend, so this was a wonderful opportunity to get to know her and learn about her work and interests. It felt like we were old friends. We had only been together for about twenty minutes when I heard her ask me if I would write a book about S.T.A.R. for her company to publish. Oh my goodness! This was too much fun. I knew that she had never received one of my query letters because they went only to agents. Something else was definitely at work on my behalf.

The universe had taken me on an amazing ride through the world of self-publishing. I had not backed down even though the way was new, foreign and definitely not of my choosing. After I got my gold stars for effort, I was gifted with a grander outcome than I had intended, a publisher that completely understood what I was saying! There were very few publishing companies in the country for which I could make that statement. My concern from the start of this whole process had been that if I had been accepted by a publishing company the editors would have asked me to change what I had to say to accommodate their readers. Ja-lene asked no such thing. (Her company closed in 2016.)

Ronna Herman says, "Focus on that which wells up within you as the most important issue of your life. Seek validation from within your Sacred Heart and from your Higher Self. Dedicate yourself to accomplishing that which you desire with all your energy—physical/mental/emotional and spiritual—until it is brought to fruition. If you have doubts, start small, until you become proficient in using your latent abilities of co-creation. Sweep aside your doubts, and do not listen to others' criticism or admonitions. Follow your own inner guidance; you will not be led astray." [7]

TRANSMITTING OUR BEINGNESS TO THE "FIELD"

My whole body had been dedicated to the intention of finding a publisher for my first book. My feelings and my thoughts were aligned and being transmitted to the field in a clear, coherent way, far beyond my ego's comprehension. We are the creators of our reality and attract to ourselves what it is that we image. When we surrender to our human divinity, trust and allow, we often receive unimaginable gifts from the universe, which sometimes we do not recognize. Being an observer of the experiences, people and material objects that come to us, we can begin to see how the field is weaving all that we need, to do all that we have dreamed. Now is the time to dream from a conscious state of being instead of allowing the subconscious to imagine with limitations.

7. Archangel Michael, channeled by Ronna Herman, *The Gathering of Souls,* www.spiritlibrary.com/ronna-herman/the-gathering-of-souls, August 1, 2012.

My experience is not unique to me. We all have access to the field in which all possibilities exist. What is your dream? Could it be to find a job where you are able to express your passion? Perhaps you imagine entering a new relationship where you are honored? What is it that would fill your heart if it were manifested and expressed?

Bring your dream and your gratitude for the manifestation of that dream together knowing that it already exists and awaits the perfect moment to be expressed. You are a unique aspect of All That Is. Why would this not be possible?

When the human and the divine are separate, sending out polar opposite signals to the field, dreams fade and imagining dissipates. Now we know that we are divine humans, not sometimes human and sometimes divine. Our wholeness, when we accept this as our truth, is then aligned with the will of the divine Creator and the field responds with "miracles." Dreams blossom and imagining soars!

Dr. Joe Dispenza says, "The quantum field doesn't respond simply to our wishes—our emotional requests. It doesn't just respond to our aims—our thoughts. It only responds when those two are aligned or coherent—that is, when they are broadcasting the same signal. When we combine an elevated emotion with an open heart and a conscious intention with clear thought, we signal the field to respond in amazing ways."[8]

A prior feeling of lack of self-worth would not have aligned with my intention and my dream would have been blocked. I would have received less than, not greater than I had imagined, which was the final outcome.

8. Dr. Joe Dispenza, *Breaking the Habit of Being Yourself: How to Lose Your Mind and Create a New One* (Carlsbad, CA: Hay House, Inc., 2012), p. 20.

Allow yourself to receive greater than you have dreamed: a job where you can express your passion and which provides you new avenues to explore and expand; a new relationship where you are not only honored but allowed to grow in ways that are encouraged. Receive with gratitude and appreciation all that awaits your dream and your choosing.

"The thoughts we think send an electrical signal out into the field. The feelings we generate magnetically draw events back to us. Together, how we think and how we feel produces a state of being, which generates an electromagnetic signature that influences every atom in our world."[9]

RECEIVE WITH APPRECIATION AND GRATITUDE WHAT WHOLENESS HAS IMAGINED AND CHOSEN.

---

9. Ibid., pp. 20, 21.

AFTER S.T.A.R. COMES ACCEPT

Surrender, trust, allow and receive, these are the basic fundamental principles of creating our desires. But if we do all this work and then close our hand or turn our back and walk away when presented with something extraordinary or miraculous, what's the point? When we get miraculous results we have to *accept* those miraculous results. Accepting is taking action, internalizing what we have received with appreciation and gratitude. Accepting new ideas attracts more new thought frequencies, which creates new circuits in the brain. Repetition increases the process and belief is established. Positive beliefs allow the flow of imagination to manifest.

THE CYCLE OF ACCEPTING NEW IDEAS

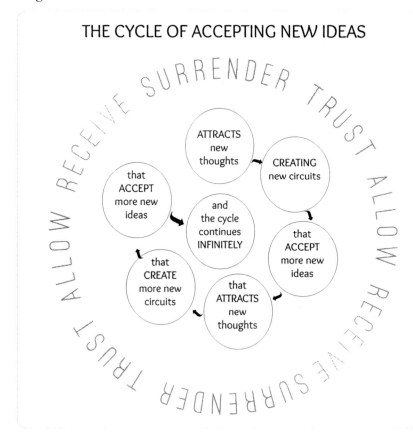

The difference between Receive and Accept can be explained by the example of receiving an invitation and then accepting that invitation.

To accept is agreeing or consenting to what has been received. We make a commitment. The thought, "I have received an invitation," is followed by a question, "Is the invitation to be accepted?" "Yes" or "No" generates an action step, which is chemically communicated to the body. When the mind and body are aligned in time and space, a new action or behavior results.

Perhaps we might receive a spontaneous idea for a new business. Will we accept? Will we act? Will we commit? The step after receiving is accepting or rejecting. With the acceptance, new experiences are allowed to present themselves, resulting in new emotions, which get fired and wired as new circuits in our brain. We have expanded our behavior and shifted our identity.

Recently a friend shared a story about an incident that changed her profoundly. A massage therapist had offered her a free massage, which she later explained was more like a Rolfing session (manipulation of the muscle fasciae). She spent a lot of time explaining how difficult it was for her to receive this gift. She had received the words about the gift but was having a difficult time accepting the gift. She wanted to pay for the session or have another creative way of providing an equal exchange. Intuitively she knew that it was important for her to accept what was being offered to her. With difficulty she said yes, but her body was still resisting. Then, when she was on the table and her muscles were being relaxed, she surrendered completely to the process, fully accepting the nurturing of her body. At that point, though painful to experience the manipulation of her muscle fasciae, she began to cry and a wave of deep knowing or secret inner truth swept through her body as if it had been unleashed. All of her resistance mechanisms had let go, and her body accepted completely the gift that she was being given—nurturing from another. She was accepting the fullest expression of that gift in her body *and* her spirit so that she could feel love and appreciation for who she was.

Another example of "receiving words" versus "accepting" them can be demonstrated when one seeks advice from a consultant. The words that are being spoken are received by the client and then the brain sorts through what is being communicated and either rejects or accepts what was shared. If an idea is accepted it is felt by the body as new truth, which may result in an action. The information, therefore, must go beyond being received for behavior or personality to shift.

 It is as if, when accepted, the words received resonate with our innate knowing, they feel like truth, and can be let in and played with. The mind and the body are accepting and allowing a new experience to be expressed.

Once we have accepted information or thoughts, and they become our truth, it then becomes easier to stand in that truth and not be influenced by one's environment or the chiding of another. I had just such an experience after I posted a message on a social media network, and to my surprise I received a negative comment. At first I was shocked and then a bit upset wondering if I had made a mistake, for apparently I had caused a strong emotional response in another. On reflection, there was nothing in my message that I would have changed. I had received and accepted the information as my truth. The reader was having his unique experience, and that was all it was. Had I just transferred information that I had received, I might have been shaken and regretted my action, but having accepted the information I had shared, the impact of the event quickly passed and was forgotten.

Just as the social media reader had a reaction to my words, so have friends reacted to the change they observed in me over the last few years as the awareness of who I know myself to be was changing. When we awaken to our human divinity, those around us will observe a different personality or identity expressing. When we fully accept that we are part of All That Is, then nothing can sway our internal knowing and external being. We can confidently allow other peoples' opinions to be their truth while living in a way that is true to our own nature. It is as if we have grown a new human divinity muscle by accepting a new truth. This new truth no longer comes from the environment, body or time that has been the primary influence. With our free will, we have simply made a different choice.

Free will is at play. After surrendering, trusting, allowing and receiving, one continues to have the free will to accept or not to accept. How is the decision to accept or reject to be made? By aligning one's will with the will of the divine Creator and then applying the elements of the S.T.A.R. philosophy, the answer that is perfect will flow with ease and grace. That is the formula for discernment.

INTEGRITY, INTENTION AND IMAGINATION

As we dream the Golden Age of Divine Love together, knowing our human divinity, loving ourselves and playing in the no time/no space of the *now* moment, there is the fourth pillar to contemplate. The Expanded Golden Rule that I briefly mentioned at the beginning of this book. It states: Do unto ALL of creation as you would have ALL of creation do unto you. Really this rule just means "to extend kindness."

I am not sure that all of my four foundational pillars (see page 23) are of equal length, breadth and strength yet. The first pillar is the acceptance and declaration that I am a divine human, an individual aspect of All That Is. The second pillar is loving myself with no limitation. The third pillar is moving out of the emotional tug of the past and the future into the calm of the *now* moment. The fourth pillar stands for treating all of creation with love and respect, which we wish for ourselves as well.

It seems to be a process in which each experience that I imagine is assisting me in achieving that goal of equilibrium. Let me share my thoughts on the stability of my fourth pillar, extending kindness to all creation.

Glenda Green shares, "Kindness is not just an act of charity to the young, the vulnerable or the needy. It is the will of God for everyone. Your goodness is strengthened through kindness. It is the will of the Father that you know and use that power, to be a wise custodian of what you have been given. Through acts of kindness your own abundance increases, for you have multiplied the ways in which your giving may be returned to you."[10]

There is no fly swatter in my house. A choice was made several years ago that I was not going to remove flies from my house in that manner. I have a blue glass and a piece of recycled 8½ x 11 paper easily at my reach when the spring arrives and other forms of created reality choose to share my nest. I still reserve my space as MY space, so there is an action step that becomes necessary when four-legged flying or crawling creatures wish to share it.

Capturing flies, moths, ants and even a brave salamander has become a bit of an art form for me. There is a sense of satisfaction when I am

---

10.   Glenda Green, *Love Without End: Jesus Speaks* (Sedona, AZ: Spiritis Publishing, 1999), p. 191.

successful, and I am able to "teach" these visitors that their space is on the other side of the walls of MY house. In my heart, I believe there is a new respect for each one of these life forms that honors that they, like me, are part of all creation.

Where my application of the Expanded Golden Rule gets a bit wobbly is when a mosquito lands on me. There is no nice thought in my head at that moment. I am thinking about this dilemma, however, and that is a good thing. Where the thought has taken me is that when I shut my eyes, the mosquito, according to my understanding of quantum physics, becomes waves of possibility.

Perhaps in the not-so-distant future, I will be able to remember the gifts that are my birthright; a form of mental physics[11] will be remembered and mastered so that I can choose to open my eyes and the mosquito will have gone. Why would this not be possible? If I am a divine human, if I can author my reality as a sovereign being from the quantum field of all possibility, then why can't I choose that the mosquito be elsewhere? The answer at the moment is that my belief that this is possible is not firmly integrated into my personality. The words, "No you can't!" still echo throughout me.

The flying creatures that I just described that disturb my sense of balance remind me of the flies that covered my face when, in 1980, I sat by a pool in Egypt. There was no remedy. Mental physics was not even a concept I had heard of, so I gave up. The flies won. I left the pool and went on to experience three events of human kindness, which exemplify the Expanded Golden Rule.

My former husband had won a trip for one, to any place in the world. He gave the gift to me. My choice of destination was Egypt, since my

---

11.   Archangel Metatron through James Tyberonn, www.earth-keeper.com/EKnews_74.htm.

uncle and aunt would be traveling there, and I thought it would be fun if I called them and asked if I could have dinner with them in Egypt. My travel agent suggested that I not just go for the weekend, but join a small tour, which I did.

The first act of kindness that I experienced was from the tour guide, who on learning that I had a few extra days in Cairo after the tour, asked me to visit his shop. When I walked through the door, I found him seated with friends having coffee. He seemed delighted to see me and asked me to join the coffee circle and to pick out anything I wished from his store as a gift from him. I remember well my shock and how I tried to process the act of receiving. I had no idea of the value of anything in his store and was so concerned that I would choose something too expensive. I went to the turquoise display and chose an oval stone with a flaw in it, hoping that the flaw would reduce the value. I later had the stone set in a ring, which today I call my friendship ring.

The second act of kindness was experienced when I hired a taxi to drive me to meet my uncle and aunt. We had about a thirty-minute drive outside of Cairo, and I was traveling alone. After I entered the cab, I remembered the advice that had been given to me that I was not to travel alone, but there I was, and I needed to get to my destination. I was aware of the driver looking at me through the mirror, and I became very uncomfortable. This happened throughout the trip. Then toward the end of the journey, when the taxi stopped at a red light, the driver rolled down his window and beckoned to a street vendor. I noticed that he purchased flowers from the woman, then turned to me and said, "These are for you. You are very beautiful."

The third act of kindness was expressed when another taxi driver I had engaged drove me to the music conservatory in Cairo. I had a letter from the Philadelphia Opera Company inviting their most talented opera singer to audition in the first Luciano Pavarotti International Voice Competition. I served as a board member of the opera company and had learned that there had been no response from the Egyptian conservatory to the invitation that had been extended, so I offered to contact the director in person. The driver had never heard of the conservatory and had a difficult time finding it. When I exited the cab, he would not take a tip from me. Instead, he got out of the cab and escorted me inside. He walked me to the office of the director and at that point, knowing that I was safe, he took the tip and departed.

 What is the most striking thing about these three acts of kindness is that after thirty years, I am still thinking about them and now have an opportunity to share my gratitude more publicly. I know that the energy of my appreciation has entered the quantum field and is being returned to each one of these Egyptians in some unknown, magical way. Each one of these experiences showed me the HEART of another person and allowed me to see beyond the perceived separateness that country, culture and appearance might have projected.

Thinking about the mosquitoes and the kindness of others is helping me to bring equilibrium to my four foundational pillars. With integrity, with intention and with imagination, I am becoming a new me NOW.

We have explored a new foundation on which to position ourselves in the new paradigm that is presenting: accepting our human divinity, having self-love, living in the now and being kind. From that foundation, we may choose to apply the S.T.A.R. philosophy by surrendering, trusting, allowing and receiving. Let us move forward and look at the science to support these assumptions and apply it to real-life situations. How does all of this work? How will our lives be different? Do we truly have tools to use to author and be responsible for our reality?

ARE WE NOW READY TO MANIFEST THE GOLDEN AGE
OF DIVINE LOVE TOGETHER?

NAVIGATING THE INFLUENCES

Why Quantum Physics is Relevant to S.T.A.R.

Over the last few years, pieces of the S.T.A.R./quantum physics puzzle have been appearing. Today they have coalesced, and my truth is that S.T.A.R. *is* quantum physics in action. The dots to be connected began to appear in the year 2000, when I asked the wise people around me to explain quantum physics. I had no idea what it was but had a quest to know, since I felt that it had something to do with my spiritual journey.

Then the book *Power vs. Force: The Hidden Determinants of Human Behavior* by David R. Hawkins, MD, PhD, became a fascination, and I realized there was a power beyond force that I could harness to manifest my reality. So, when I was asked by James F. Jereb to assist with the expansion of Stardreaming in 2007, I accepted on the condition that I would ask for nothing. My feeling was that if I was aligned with the will of the divine Creator, all that I would need would be provided. Many of my friends know this as my "sitting in my red leather chair" phase. Sure enough, on two occasions I was asked by strangers whom I had just met and who wished to assist me, "What do you need financially to fulfill your vision?" They were offering to assist me, and I had not asked either of them for financial assistance.

Another book that was having a profound influence on me at this time was *Love Without End: Jesus Speaks* by Glenda Green. My pencil and I read the book slowly three times. The concept of adamantine particles or particles of creation and infinity space expanded my understanding of creation.

Glenda Green explains, "There is a matrix of potential that precedes all energy mass. Its particle units are utterly generic in nature, and are the basic, irreducible components of physical existence."[12]

Having been introduced to the acronym S.T.A.R. by James and Stardreaming, I understood that surrendering our intention into the space between the particles of creation would have a magical power over the particles to move them into manifest form. I understood that was how I created my reality. My thoughts were impacting the field. I still did not know the term quantum field (discrete units of energy). That was to come four years later.

In the spring of 2012, I was creating the first S.T.A.R. clinic and identifying those individuals who would present and what would be presented. The creation of the first of anything is fascinating, since there are no tools or models from which one can lean how to proceed. All I knew, as I began the dreaming, was that the S.T.A.R. clinic was a gift to humanity from inter-dimensional/inter-galactic forces to assist in knowing our divinity. This gift was anchored in 2007 and was to be expressed in the physical in 2012, when the love frequency on the planet was sufficient to receive it.

My intuition told me that quantum physics was an important component for the first clinic, but I did not know any quantum physicists and if I did, would they be aligned with the message of the S.T.A.R. clinic, "Know Thyself as Divine?" I went searching through a stack of DVDs I had collected about science and consciousness and saw that one presenter was a theoretical quantum physicist. Wow, he even had written a book called *Quantum Doctor: A Quantum Physicist Explains the Healing Power of Integral Medicine.* I checked my inner compass and reached out

---

12. Glenda Green, *Love Without End: Jesus Speaks* (Sedona, AZ: Spiritus Publishing, 1999), p. 48.

to Dr. Amit Goswami, who had the March dates available and said yes to joining us as a principal presenter.

Best that I read his books if he was to be presenting. Wow, there it was, the connection between S.T.A.R. and quantum physics! The answer had been with me the whole time. I just had not known the science behind what I was doing as a manifestor. By surrendering my intentions into the space of infinity, I had been moving the energy of my thoughts into the quantum field as energetic waves of possibility. By trusting and allowing my human divinity aligned with the will of the divine Creator to express and expand, my vision in wave state was being collapsed into particle form so that I could receive with appreciation and gratitude. S.T.A.R. truly became for me quantum physics in action.

DREAMING OUR NEW REALITY INTO BEING

As we become clear about the deeper aspects of S.T.A.R. and how they work in union, it is natural to start re-dreaming our dreams. What do we want? How do we access the now moment of no time/no space? How do we manifest the new now?

The most fundamental idea underlying the principle of manifestation, presented in the voluminous works of Dr. Amit Goswami, is that consciousness, which he posits is the ground of all being, has a non-material component which is separate from matter. Matter is contained in consciousness.

Behind each individual expression of consciousness is what I have heard Dr. Goswami refer to as "the I behind the eye." This non-local, transcendent One Consciousness is the consciousness that chooses, in the appearance of the individuated consciousness, or the self. The non-local (transcendent) consciousness, or the One Consciousness that governs all of creation, is the causal power that can effect change. We, as divine humans, can effect positive change when we raise our frequency to a higher spiritual level and align our will with the will of the divine Creator. What kind of change is being suggested? We know that in linear 3D reality, matter can effect change; we can mow the lawn and the grass gets shorter. We can take specific ingredients, stick them in the oven and a cake is the result.

 The change that is being referred to is transcendent change exemplified by the concept of a quantum leap.

A simple review of a quantum leap is the situation when an electron in an outer orbit of an atom moves mysteriously to the inner orbit of that same atom. It did not travel from one location to another, it simply appeared. How might this relate to synchronicity, coincidence or miracles and magic?

An old energy definition of magic is "human control of supernatural agencies or the forces of nature." The new energy definition of magic is "the divine human's command of the unified energy field by means of choice." Magic is, therefore, the outcome of S.T.A.R.

I have manifested so much in my life and this phenomenon or magic is occurring more and more often and with less and less time in between occurrences. Perhaps this has always been the case, but I have not been as aware as I am today. Here is a mysterious example from my own experience, about which you may use your own discernment.

One spring day five years ago, I was wearing a pendant on a circular wire around my neck. The pendant was in the shape of a heart and was made of smokey topaz. It was one of the items that I had been gifted when my sister, Alix, entered the Carmelite Monastery and gave up all possessions. Because on that day I had misunderstood that the golf lesson I had subscribed to was on a golf course and not in a classroom, I was definitely over dressed for the morning instruction. On the drive home, I realized that the clasp on the circular wire had come undone and the pendant was missing. I was heartbroken. I returned to the golf course to look for the pendant. I searched the car. I put my hands down my shirt. I did everything I could think of to discover the new whereabouts of my symbolic memory of my sister.

At the time, I was living in a small, New Mexico, adobe (mud brick) casita. In the evening, my habit was to place my clothes on a chair in the long, narrow closet before I went to bed. They were properly placed there when I awoke the next morning. When I went to get the items that I would wear again that day, I found that right in the center, on the very top of the pile of clothes was my topaz heart. Magic? Oversight? Quantum Leap? This event would have less importance in my life if it had been a single occurrence, but it was not.

On that occasion, my intention had combined with my feelings in such a powerful way that I believe the field responded and effected transcendental change. When we consciously combine our intention and feelings and apply the principles of manifestation, which I describe as S.T.A.R., the One Consciousness, expressing through the divine human, effects change in matter that is beyond linear, third-dimensional under-standing. The particles of creation, which exist in waves of possibility, are collapsed by the divine human in ways that we might refer to as magic, but is it?

Infinity II —Love

Painting by James F. Jereb, PhD © 2010

Dr. Goswami explains, "In silence in a state of choice-less awareness, having prepared and incubated our intention, the manifestation appears by means of a quantum leap of thought or sudden insight."[13] Dr. Goswami outlines steps similar to those as proposed by this author:

DR. GOSWAMI	BROWN
Preparation	Surrender
Incubation	Trust
Sudden Insight	Allow
Manifestation	Receive

In each of these four steps, intention is joined with consciousness and energy in a state of total detachment, from the belief that the current reality is all there is, to the knowing that Source expressing through the divine human is All That Is. The next step is to take action. One possible action step is to join in community with like-minded people.

To dream the new ways of being on earth into manifest form, we need the power of community, a relationship in which we each hold a common or correlated (parallel relationship) intention. The creative solutions for life on earth will have to be inventive projects that include groups of people actively practicing surrender, trust, allow and receive. By practicing S.T.A.R., we reach a pinnacle where simultaneously each divine human is in alignment with Source. Connected in this precious

---

13.   Amit Goswami, PhD, "Scientific Evidence for the Existence of God," *The Visionary, Issue 62*, The Message Company, CineVision Productions, www. bizspirit.com, 2009.

and powerful way, we can also access octaves of wisdom and discernment—this gives us an opportunity to imagine and then actually accept what once was just a dream or a fleeting ideal. These new solutions will be translated by the personality and the new insights made into new brain circuits, so that "we can dance with God"[14] in the manifested way of being on the earth.

Perhaps one choice for the new earth might be that shared in 1924 by Baird T. Spalding in *Life and Teaching of the Masters of the Far East*:

"There is a striking resemblance between the life and teaching of Jesus of Nazareth and those of these Masters (of the Far East) as exemplified in their daily life. It has been thought impossible for man to derive his daily supply directly from the Universal, to overcome death and to perform the various so-called miracles that Jesus performed while on earth. The Masters prove that all these are their daily life. They supply everything needed for their daily wants directly from the Universal, including food, clothing and money. They have so far overcome death that many of them now living are over five hundred years of age, as was conclusively proved by their records."[15]

Imagine and accept what once were just dreams or fleeting ideals.

Could the new physics of the new earth be non-linear mental physics, the influence of precise thought upon matter? Is this what is our birthright? Is it what the Masters of the Far East knew? Imagine that we are that masterful as well, and we have merely forgotten.

---

14. Ibid.

15. Baird T. Spalding, *Life and Teaching of the Masters of the Far East*, Volume I (Marina del Rey, CA: DeVorss & Co., 1924), p. 13.

CREATING NEW WAYS OF BEING ON EARTH

Changing our choices means we can start to imagine things beyond the box of our known reality and create new ways of being on earth. How does one do that when they have never experienced what is beyond the limits of their personal box? S.T.A.R. is the answer. One surrenders the energy of their intention, expressing as waves of possibility, trusting these waves will travel beyond the experiences of the personality, allowing their divinity to create in the field of the unknown where all possibilities exist. Then, one receives that which has been collapsed into particle form or manifested by one's will being in alignment with the will of the divine Creator. We then receive with the emotions of appreciation and gratitude.

Perhaps further review of quantum physics will assist in the understanding of these concepts. The first premise is that matter is NOT a fundamental property of quantum physics as it is in Newtonian physics. Dr. Goswami writes, "There is (not) an objective reality 'out there' independent of consciousness...the universe is 'self-aware' and...it is consciousness itself that creates the physical world."[16]

The second premise is that matter is energy that exists in discrete units, quanta, which can appear as both waves (waves of possibilities) and particles (localized objects). The third premise is that observing the wave collapses it into a particle. The fourth premise, again according to Dr. Goswami, is that it is consciousness (distinguished from the mind) that collapses the wave function to create the material world. The material world is created by the downward causation of the One Consciousness, which collapses the wave potential into a particle or material event. Thus the *observer* creates or projects reality. The Observer is the observed. The

---

16. Amit Goswami, PhD, *The Self-Aware Universe: How Consciousness Creates the Material World* (New York, NY: Tarcher/Putnam, 1993), p. xv.

fifth premise is that since matter is energy, everything in the quantum universe is connected.

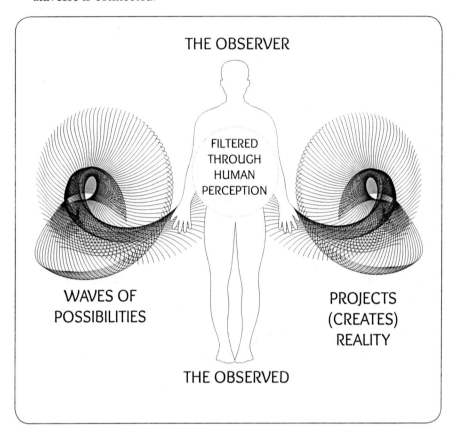

Only our wholeness can re-calibrate our choices or create an unknown reality. To do this, we must trust and allow our human divinity, not our ego/personality, to collapse the waves of possibilities into particles of localized objects—in doing so our experiences are greatly enhanced. To do this we must remember who we truly are. Once we know our human divinity, then S.T.A.R. becomes the magic wand which empowers us to shift from the old energy of only creating the known within the box to the new expanded energy of creating the unknown, outside of the box with ease and grace.

Dr. Dispenza explains that when we "apply" our will to our mind to think outside the box (dream or imagine), it forces the brain to fire in new sequences and combinations thus causing the nerve cells that have been wired together to re-pattern, allowing the brain and the body to change to become a map of the future. In other words, the environment is an extension of our mind. When we change our mind, our life changes. A process of inner alchemy has occurred, which is mirrored on the outside as a new way of being on the earth.

Now that we have used physics "to demystify the mystical,"[17] how do we want our creation to express? As creator beings connected to the One Consciousness or heartbeat of Source, let us imagine together what might be possible in the yet unknown existence of a new way of being on the earth. All we need do is dream it together for it to express and expand.

Seeds of NOW in the Media

Are we changing our choices about media already? If so, what a powerful way to effect consciousness on the planet.

How many hours do we focus on television, theater and film? Whatever the number is, it is a lot and those hours catch our attention powerfully. These are seeds of thought, transmitted to the collective, that possess immense, potential spiritual knowledge. For example, let's look at the movie *Avatar*. According to one internet search, domestic lifetime gross receipts were $760,507,625.[18] It takes a lot of people to have that revenue figure, and we did not consider DVD sales. *The Matrix*

---

17.   Dr. Joe Dispenza, *Evolve Your Brain: The Science of Changing Your Mind*, www.youtube.com/watch?v=VMN_Sd9qdIE.

18.   www.boxofficemojo.com, updated 11/18/2012.

had domestic total gross revenue of $171,479,930.[19]

What are the subtle messages that are being received from these seeds of thought? With *Avatar*, we are introduced to the concept that all of creation is interconnected. We witness this when the Na'vi who inhabit the earth-like moon, Pandora, are weakened when their ecology is destroyed by human invaders. With *The Matrix*, one seed message is that all life on earth may be nothing more than an elaborate facade or illusion. We witness this when Neo is introduced to Morpheus who sheds light on the dark.

One of my favorite movies is *The Blue Bird*[20] with Elizabeth Taylor and Eva Gardner. Mytyl and her brother Tyltyl are peasant children who meet the Queen of Light and are instructed to seek the Blue Bird of Happiness. They are given a hat with a magic diamond, which when turned calls forth the souls of living and inanimate things. The human personifications of water, fire, light, a cat and a dog join them on the journey. They eventually discover that the Blue Bird of Happiness is to be found at home.

In *The Blue Bird* the human personification of water and fire gave me a keener sense of what I often take for granted, that inanimate objects are aspects of All That Is and are to be honored and appreciated as part of all creation. The message for me was that my life's journey of seeking outside of myself comes full circle in the realization that the Blue Bird of Happiness is to be found within.

I wish to acknowledge the courageous media pioneers who risk their reputations and careers by creating the new and telling a different story.

---

19. www.boxofficemojo.com, updated 11/18/2012.

20. *The Blue Bird*, 20th Century Fox, 1976.

INFLUENTIAL SYSTEMS

What would the systems, which control our everyday existence, become in a new way of being on earth? Could we choose to redirect the energy of mega-economic systems to support a kinder, gentler world simply by imagining and dreaming different choices? Again, all change begins with our own inner alchemy, and that change is reflected in our environment. Systems will not change until we change our choices.

Is it already occurring? An antisocial college student founded Facebook, which went from zero to reaching BILLIONS in four years. He created a new system that virtually every large business in the world has been forced to use to remain competitive. Facebook has changed the election process and been the communication device that gathered people together to create a revolution and right the "wrongs" of the world. That is system change.

Email and search engines have provided a mighty tool to communicate across borders and research in minute detail what has previously been information available to the few. We are connected in a web of communication that is requiring a transparency of right action from those who have believed that no one would notice.

We are beginning to take responsibility and to realize that we can effect change. What more can we dream into reality?

RECONSIDERING WELLNESS

What would wellness look like? What do we want it to look like? This too is our choice. Scout Cloud Lee in her book *Shazam! The Formula* has a simple solution. On receiving the news that she had terminal cancer and two months to live, she made the choice to "Focus on living my life rather than planning for my death." Scout has lived 22 years past that diagnosis.

 Are we so patterned and conditioned that our identity is defined by an illness or the suffering we are enduring? When we can move beyond the diagnosis and into imagining new possibilities, everything shifts. Do we have the divine will to create a new identity, which removes the conditions that have had power over us?

Could the switch to wellness be as simple as choice? If so, who is making the choice, our ego self or our divine self? In Buddhism, the new identity and new consciousness, which takes back power, is called *no self*.

Anam Thubten writes, "When the awakening happens, there is no longer any desire to become someone other than who we are. Every previous idea of who we are vanishes and along with it the pain, guilt, and pride associated with our body. In Buddhism this is called *no self*."[21]

The new identity of the *no self*, which I call human divinity, has an awakened remembering that one can go inside one's physical body to communicate an intention for healing and that the consciousness of the body's multi-dimensional DNA field will listen. In Lee Carroll's recent book, *The Twelve Layers of DNA (An Esoteric Study of the Mastery Within)*, we are reminded that the "junk DNA" that surrounds our double helix genetic codes, which according to Dr. Todd Ovokaitys comprises 97% of the entire human code, contains a system of twelve energies or layers.

---

21. Anan Thubten, *No Self, No Problem* (Ithaca, NY: Snow Lion Publications, 1973), p. 3.

It "carries within it more than 100,000 years of 'who you might be.'"[22] This non-coded junk DNA is the real energy of our spirituality or the multi-dimensional instructions for the coded DNA.

For the "junk DNA" to be the energy of our spirituality, it would have to have consciousness, and thus we come to what humanity has forgotten for eons. Our multi-dimensional DNA field wants to communicate with us. "Without us 'talking' to our cells...DNA is just resting, doing the automatic things within our body. DNA is always listening...Therefore, it's our job to inform our own DNA what we need...the key to change in the Human body is *information*, not chemistry."[23]

It is as if we have been a passenger on our own bus, which is being driven on auto-pilot. The time is now to sit in the driver's seat and give the commands. What do you dream? Tell your multi-dimensional DNA field your instructions. Who are you? Why can't you do this if you are a divine human? Give the instructions then move into S.T.A.R. and let go of the outcome. Communicate an intention for wellness to the multi-dimensional DNA field, and we remove the need for illness from the new earth.

Could it be that illness is a gift of the divine for us to ultimately surrender to the knowing that we are divine humans and that at that point, illness no longer has power over us? Should that become our truth, then the gift of illness is no longer needed. We are indeed moving into a new way of being on earth where we can declare that illness and suffering have served their purpose and may now pass on.

As we begin to remember how to communicate with our multi-

---

22. Lee Carroll, *The Twelve Layers of DNA (An Esoteric Study of the Mastery Within)*, Kryon Book Twelve (Sedona, AZ: Platinum Publishing House, 2010), p. 23.

23. Ibid., p. 76.

dimensional DNA field, we might instruct it to return to its original blueprint, the 100% perfect intrauterine DNA, which existed before birth. According to Kryon, via Lee Carroll, since we were born with free choice, at birth we begin to experience the energies on the planet and our DNA begins to alter.

One might ask with this knowing, "Why do I have to grow old?" In our creation of the new earth, would it not be possible to instruct our genes to get stronger instead of weaker? We have been told that weaker is the natural progression of one's life. Could we not instruct the regenerating cells in our body to remember their perfected state instead of atrophying? Will we be creating new actuarial life tables, which recalculate life expectancy? Perhaps.

PURE PROSPERITY

Will daily existence be a struggle or could we dream into existence all that we need to support us in achieving that which we came to earth to accomplish? Will what is manifested always be the comfort that the personality struggles for? What is the definition of prosperity in the new way of being on earth? One way to find the answer might be to project oneself to the last day of physical expression on the planet. When we have the vantage point of looking back, what do we hold as valuable? Would it be the money that we have earned? Would it be the "stuff" that we have collected? Perhaps not, perhaps we might hold most valuable the relationships with our family, friends and neighbors and the experiences through which we have traveled.

My personal story illustrating prosperity and what I hold valuable occurred during the summer of 2010. I was standing on the second-floor terrace overlooking the Sangre de Cristo Mountains in Santa Fe. My home is perhaps five miles away from the southernmost sub-range of the Rocky Mountains. The mountains have twelve thousand foot peaks, which are what I see when I wake up in the morning. The Spanish name, meaning "blood of Christ," is said to come from the red color of the range at some sunrises and sunsets, especially when the mountains are covered with snow, alpenglow.

This particular July morning, I could smell and see smoke coming off the mountain range from the backside. The fire was in the Pueblo of Nambé, just north of Santa Fe. The dry weather had caused yet another fire in New Mexico, but this one was close to my home. As I stood there, I imagined the pine and aspen trees catching on fire fed by the brittle floor matting. Fires spread easily and are difficult to control during our frequent periods of drought.

My mind went to the trip I was to take that day to Cape May, New Jersey, to join my family for a holiday. With my eldest son's family living in Brussels, Belgium, my daughter's family in Millis, Massachusetts, and my youngest son in Gainesville, Georgia, distance and varying school schedules make it difficult for us to gather together very often. This trip, therefore, was very important to me. The question on my mind was, should I stay or should I go? Was I to remain at home to protect it? Was I to grab my treasures and move them to a safe location?

What do you treasure?

These thoughts had occurred to me before, for I believe there is a fear of fire that resides deep within my cellular memory. I can tell you of the "things" that I had thought of saving, when the fear had entered my mind in the past. This day was different. I was different. What I heard myself saying in the depths of my inner being, was, "No things matter.

87

They do not define me. I have been without before. What matters is me, my well-being and my family. No things will keep me from being with those I love. I am going no matter what happens to my house."

Another story might be helpful in finding the definition of prosperity, which so often is associated with material success. In April, 1995, when living in Philadelphia, Pennsylvania, I was the subject of a cover story in *Business Philadelphia Magazine*: "She's Got Money! Nina Brown has collateral funding for women-owned businesses. It's about time." The words that were written were correct. Our new company, Women's Collateral Funding, had raised enough money to fund two women-owned businesses with a new funding instrument that we created, venture collateral. What no one had asked me was if *I* had any money.

The truth was that I had put so much of my personal time, effort and money behind the creation of this pioneering company that I did not have the funds to pay for the hotel room in Harrisburg so that I could accept an award from the governor of Pennsylvania.

So what is the definition of success or prosperity? I was changing the country's opinion of the newly emerging market of women entrepreneurs, but I was not making money at it. Money is so often a measurement for success. This query perplexed me for years.

Did I have to receive money to prove my value? When my bank account was empty, was I prosperous? The answer came to me as I moved into the S.T.A.R. philosophy; I am successful when my will is aligned with the will of the divine Creator. This is the new way of being on earth in prosperity.

BALANCE AND EQUILIBRIUM

In the new way of being on earth, would we disrespect other living creatures for our own gain or would we choose balance and equilibrium (or moderation) as our way of co-existing with other aspects of All That Is? Is it conceivable to imagine a life without war? Because war has always been a condition of human experience, does that mean that it always has to be? What if we choose peace? Could it be that simple? Does the new way of being on earth mean living in harmony with all of creation? Would global exchange of resources, land and assets be based on "what's in it for me?" or would we recognize those individuals, with different features and cultures, as being yet another mirror of ourselves and therefore choose to adopt an exchange governed by the principles of mutual consent?

What do we want the new earth, the Golden Age of Divine Love to be like? Perhaps all we need to do is imagine it, choose it and manifest it by means of S.T.A.R. How, we might ask? Come together in love to imagine is my answer. "When two or more are gathered..."

Let us dream together in the field of infinite possibilities!

When we dream together, the field of infinite possibilities is vast and so much richer than when we dream alone. Gather in small groups with common purpose. Gather in large groups in silence with coherent thought. Surrender to the intention to call in the new, the unknown Golden Age of Divine Love. Trust that, aligned with the will of the divine Creator, the waves of energy potential emitted into the quantum field will express. Together, allow the dreaming to expand beyond the known into the field of the unknown. Then together, receive with appreciation and gratitude what is collapsed into particle form, in alignment with the One Consciousness, as our new way of being on earth, the Golden Age of Divine Love. Then together we can play with our new awareness.

HOW DO WE GET TO NOW?

Now is play. When I give this special definition, people often look quite puzzled. To play is to be in the now moment of no time/no space. Have you ever asked yourself, "What does 'to play' mean?" What does it mean when my grandson says to me, "I want to go out and play?" Play what? He is not referring to soccer or cards. He just wants to play.

On reflection, over many months of asking for the definition of play, it came to me that play is defined as: being in the now. So, what does play look like for adults when they are not actively involved in a game of play? Can we be playing while sitting on the porch looking at our flowers? Can we be at play when we are visiting a friend, shopping, at the bank or working at our job?

The answer is yes, on all of those occasions we can be in the now, being completely engaged in the creativity of the moment with no attachments, memories or patterns from the past controlling our thoughts. We can be so immersed in the flow of the moment, outside of our environment, our personality and time that we connect with the quantum (discrete energy) field of all possibilities, from which we can choose new thoughts or their resulting experience with joy and appreciation, the feeling of play.

How does one move their awareness into the play time of now when we have real-world obligations? Got to go to work. Got to make supper for my kids. Need food. Need shelter. Need clothing. The car has to be fixed. My mom needs me because she is very ill. When things like this do happen in our lives, we wonder, "How can I create play time when I have so many *have to's*?"

PLAY IS SACRED

SURRENDER · TRUST · ALLOW · RECEIVE · SURRENDER · TRUST · ALLOW · RECEIVE

COLOR
GO ✧ PRETEND
TRAVEL ✧ MARVEL
EXPLORE ✧ DISCOVER
DANCE ✧ PAINT ✧ COOK ✧ PARTY
DECORATE ✧ DREAM ✧ SHOP
GARDEN ✧ SING ✧ PLAY GAMES
LISTEN ✧ BE CURIOUS ✧ SEE MOVIES
VISIT STRANGE PLACES ✧ LAUGH
WALK BAREFOOT
TAKE PICTURES
DAYDREAM

When we approach our work and obligations as play, the behaviors instantly shift. I like to think of the Japanese tea ceremony or the Zen gardens and remember with what focus and attention each movement is made. There is love being expressed for each object and for each action. One of my dreams is that I come to a state of being where I have such respect for all of creation. A way that I am being that conscious is the first thing in the morning when I move my feet over the side of the bed. Instead of just jumping out and rushing off to begin my day, I take a moment. The act of touching the floor is done consciously. It is as if I am acknowledging that I am moving into the waking reality of the day and asking permission to play with whatever is to appear until I choose to move into dream state again.

When grown-ups play, they only have to ask themselves for permission.

Should that day present challenges, perhaps I will have enough quiet time to review my past and to identify similar events where I felt trapped or at a loss. With hindsight, I have the privilege of observing whom I became as a result of those experiences. This reflection will help steady me during that day's challenges. My life has been richly filled with life-changing episodes—wealth, lack, joy, pain, health, illness... With honesty, I can say that I am grateful for each emotion and each way of expressing, for without all of these ways of being, I would not be who I am today. I know that there are more experiences to come, and they may not be comfortable. I do change when I am uncomfortable. How do I want to be? What events will move me into that state of being? Do I fear what is to come? Or is it all perfect?

What would make me fear what is to come is allowing myself to step out of the now moment and to pull in old thoughts, old beliefs, old ways of being, to influence the present. When I stay focused on the cup as I am pouring the Japanese green tea, then that is all there is and it is perfect just as it is.

When we are in the now, we are not thinking about the events of the past that cause painful emotions and their correlating behavior. Our thoughts are disengaged from old patterns and ways of being. We are allowing our mind and our body to create new brain circuits and wir-ings to break old connections to create the new. We tap into the field of quantum energy potential that gives us joy and appreciation, the emotions of play.

The science behind disengaging from past, present or future thoughts, feelings and behavior is meticulously explained by Dr. Dispenza in *Break-ing the Habit of Being You*: the key to change is breaking subconscious pat-terns. The brain and the rest of the body create corresponding chemicals that are released when one has a thought resulting in a feeling. Over time, the body memorizes the feeling response and develops an addiction for the resulting chemical. Behavior is influenced by the memorized feeling and this becomes one's state of being or personality. Our bodies are nourished by the memory of suffering, as an example, because of the chemical that it releases. To break this subconscious pattern, we need to change our thoughts and simultaneously our feelings, which disrupt the circuits that have become wired together.

"The main obstacle to breaking the habit of being yourself is thinking and feeling *equal* to your environment, your body, and time... learning to think and feel (be) *greater than* the 'Big Three' [environment, body and time] is your first goal as you prepare..."[24]—I would add, to create a new you. Thinking alone is not sufficient. One must think (caused by the environ-ment), feel (the body's reaction to thought) and have or imagine "greater than" current experiences for new circuits to be created in the brain. This must happen outside of time or in the now with no chemical charge from thoughts of the past, present or future. When we dream a creative thought and imagine what it would feel like, we have released ourselves from time and begun to live in the now, the quantum field of all possibilities.

---

24. Dr. Joe Dispenza, *Breaking the Habit of Being Yourself: How to Lose Your Mind and Create a New One* (Carlsbad, CA: Hay House, Inc., 2012), p. 94.

Detach from Suffering from the Past

The S.T.A.R. state of being is living in the now. How do we get there when we are attached to memories of suffering from the past that pull on us? The answer is, we must "do the work." Each one of those memories is simply an experience teaching us a life lesson. We are not served by carrying them forward as emotionally charged events. We are on the planet to experience so that we can grow on the spiral of life in consciousness. Life presents us constantly with experiences through which we learn. Where we are held back is when we can't let go of the emotions that accompany the memory of those events, somewhat like the dependency on a drug. We become addicted, as Dr. Dispenza suggests, to the neuropeptides that each emotion produces. Therefore, we may find our self in a completely difference circumstance and react to it based on old emotional programming and the judgment that was remembered and associated with that memory.

Detaching from the addiction of debilitating emotions is necessary for us to move into the now with ease and grace. Inner alchemy work is the answer. There are many ways in which one can accomplish this clearing, but the most powerful is intention or choosing. Let me share my story with you as an example. The event occurred before I had any awareness of S.T.A.R. It was the intuitive beginning of walking down that new road.

In 1993, I met a man who suggested that I attend a three-day workshop sponsored by Landmark Education. I had no idea what the weekend conference he had suggested was about, but I trusted his recommendation. One evening before the event, the phone rang. The caller identified herself as staff for the Forum, the conference I was to attend. She wanted to know what I wanted to accomplish over the three-day period. What?

No one had prepared me for that question, but I heard myself listing three things that I wished to resolve.

1. *Peace with my deceased alcoholic mother*

2. *Peace with my cloistered Carmelite nun sister*

3. *Peace with my husband, whom I was divorcing*

These were the three major events in my life causing me to experience suffering from the past. At the time, I was engulfed with self-pity for all that I was enduring from each one of those relationships. There was no blueprint that I could find for a resolution. Without going into the details of what I believed each family member had "done to me," I now choose not to give power to the events by describing them as I used to remember them. The core issue with each situation stemmed from a perceived feeling of isolation, abandonment and ultimately lack of self-worth. It was easy to blame my mother, sister and husband for being the cause of those negative emotions.

My mother, Lanta, was an elegant Philadelphia lady who taught me graciousness and style. She was born into a middle-class family from a small town in Delaware. After she came to Philadelphia to study nursing, she met and married my father and quickly learned the fine qualities of proper society. Toward the end of her life, alcohol became her best friend, which also caused a shift in her personality. My relationship with mother had always been strained, but it completely dissolved at the time of her death. I could not stand to look at an image of her, so the photos were packed in a box in my basement.

My sister, Alix, was my idol as I was growing up. Her love for me, her elegance and the fact that she was my only sibling caused me to want to show her off to all of my friends. She is four years older than me and has always held a special place in my heart, perhaps even more so because mother did not. When she went to study painting in Italy during her college years, she chose to convert her religious affiliation from being an Episcopalian to being a Catholic. Then shortly after her conversion, she traveled thirteen hours from her apartment in Florence, Italy, to San Giovanni Rotondo to attend Mass with Padre Pio, a Capuchin Catholic priest, who is now venerated as a saint in the Catholic Church. While in prayer, she instantly knew that she wanted to choose a life as a consecrated religious. In her search for the order to join, she read a biography of St. Teresa of Avila and knew that she was to join the Carmelite order. She took her vow of poverty in June of 1964. I spent the next thirty years grieving the loss of my sister, Alix, who had transformed into the cloistered nun, Sister Pia of Christ Crucified.

My former husband, Grant, had a stellar career as a Philadelphia lawyer and was an expert in medical malpractice law defending doctors and hospitals. He loved to cook and arrange flowers, so he displayed both an academic and an artistic nature. He too found in alcohol relief from stress. After his second major episode, I asked for a divorce. The thought of how I was going to make a living did not enter into my thinking. I just knew that we could not continue as a married couple.

My mother, my sister and my husband were the focus of my weekend at the Forum, though they did not hold my full attention. The work that was presented to us was all-consuming and demanding. It called for a great deal of introspection in a very short period of time. The moment of my life-changing experience came when one of the instructors told me that "grief is words unspoken," and that those unspoken words were, "I love you." I asked if one could speak the words to someone who was deceased and the answer was, "Yes."

I could hardly wait until the Sunday lunch break to tell my deceased mother that I loved her. How I was going to do that was not clear immediately. When the awaited time came, I went to the parking lot and got into my old car, a white Honda. Sitting quietly for a bit, it occurred to me to say the Lord's Prayer. Then I called on the spirit of my mother. Almost immediately, I felt her presence. My father was present as well. Out of my mouth came the simple words, "I love you." Then it occurred to me to kiss the etheric presence of my mother, which I did. A peace came over me, as I sat quietly in my car, until it was time to resume our work. When I drove home that evening after the completion of the weekend, I knew that my mother's spirit was with me. I immediately went down into the basement and retrieved a photograph of her that was in an old silver frame. I placed it prominently on a mahogany table, next to the couch in my living room.

A simple, sincere "I love you" is more transformational than forgiveness.

The next day, Monday, I called Grant and asked if I could see him. Then I called the Carmelite Monastery and told the message machine that I would be coming to visit Sister Pia. Grant appeared at my doorstep soon afterwards. He did not choose to enter my townhouse, so we stayed on the front porch. I looked deeply into his eyes and said, "Grant, I need to tell you that I love you." The words or events that followed are not clear to me, but there was definitely a shift. It was as if any bitterness I had toward my husband slipped away. I saw my then ex-husband a few years later at the wedding of our daughter. He was sitting behind me with his two sisters. I remember feeling at ease in his presence and turning around to greet him. Both of his sisters commented afterwards how nice it was to see my warm greeting of their brother.

When the day came that I was to visit Sister Pia, I was told to sit in the very sterile "speak room." My sister opened up the wooden screen that separated us. I could see her, behind the upright metal bars, dressed as usual in the brown and white clothing that she wore representing her order. Her skin was tight with no wrinkles and her cheeks, as always, were rosy and beautiful. Everyone who sees her goes away knowing that she is truly happy with the choice that she made at such a young age. I stood up and approached the barrier between us. I took her hands and looked her in the eyes. "I love you" came easily out of my mouth. Then I gestured that I wanted to kiss her through the bars. When we were complete, she said, "I have been waiting for you to tell me that." I left the convent in peace.

My goal had been accomplished, I was at peace with my mother, my husband and my sister and it happened by means of changing my mind and speaking three short words, "I love you," to each one of my family members. The power that my suffering had over me disappeared. Perhaps what occurred was a quantum leap. It felt as if the weight that had been on my shoulders had melted away. I was lighter and felt free.

 The suffering I had known has never returned, and I am in balance with all the people in my life because, with the wisdom of time, I have come to know that the way that a person expresses themselves through their personality, is not who they are. They too are divine humans.

At her essence, my mother was not a woman of society who drank to escape her loneliness. She was and is an enormous being of light who chose to experience incarnation under those conditions. My sister is not a devout, cloistered nun, whom I see rarely. She is an enormous being of light who chose to experience incarnation under those conditions.

My now deceased ex-husband was not a successful attorney who chose scotch over his family and clients. He was and is an enormous being of light who chose to experience incarnation under those conditions.

The shift that occurred for me was experienced as a result of an intention or choice. There was never an act of forgiveness, just love. There are currently few ties to the past that keep me from living my life in the now. My method of change or inner alchemy may not be yours. It matters not. What does matter is that we do the work, in whatever way is our path, into the now.

Dr. Joe Dispenza tells us: "If we have experienced suffering, and within our minds and bodies we hold that suffering and express it through our thoughts and feelings, we broadcast that energetic signature into the field. The universal intelligence responds by sending into our lives another event that will reproduce the same intellectual and emotional response."[25]

What I had done was change the cycle of thinking, feeling, and acting in the same way that I had done for years by changing the underlying emotion to pure love. The memorized habitual response was disempowered. The neural circuitry was rewired. I was free and grateful to the instructor, whose name I don't remember, for changing my life in one weekend and allowing me to detach from the suffering I had known from the past.

Is there a gift in this knowing that I might be able to give to the reader so that you might see a way to detach from the emotions of the past? The most important thought that comes to me is, "It is all about you." Each experience in life is created or attracted to us so that we can move through it into a new way of being. How am I speaking in this experience? Am I making another person wrong? How am I listening in

---

25. Ibid., p. 29.

this experience? Am I hearing with focused attention? How am I acting in this experience? Am I filled with grace in the presence of others? How am I being in this experience? We tend to analyze how the other person is being, speaking and listening. All that matters is you in each now moment. Would you be proud to stand in the presence of the masters, being who you are in this moment? You too are a master. Would you be proud of yourself? If not, choose another way of being. It is that simple. As we choose another way of being, we impact the field around us. The experience shifts as we shift.

DETACH FROM FEAR OF THE FUTURE

The future is the unknown, the uncontrollable realm of our projections. Will I get that job? How can I do what they are asking of me? Will I be able to pay the mortgage next month? These and many more unanswerable questions swim around unpredictably in our future concept of time. Add to those concerns our memory of expectations unattained from when we have tried to forecast the future many times in our life.

How are we expected to focus our attention on the now when we have anxiety about the next step on our journey? We must be in control. That idea has been taught to us since we were young and our personality reinforces that belief. What do you want to be when you grow up? Be sure to marry the right person so that you...Plan for the future. Do retirement planning or you will be poor when you are old because Social Security is running out of money.

I have been there. Here is my story. Most of my life, I have given food or money to the needy at Thanksgiving. However, my memory of Thanksgiving Day in 2000, is of being on the verge of losing my apartment, having my telephone service disconnected, seeing my rental furniture repossessed and of a friend bringing me a simple Thanksgiving dinner. This could have been a profound moment for me to feel fear of the future. At the time, I simply had an innate knowing that my life circumstances did not define who I was. This knowing influenced my exterior reality over time and that state of being in lack turned around. Self-pity and focus on my hardship might have perpetuated that condition.

One tool that we as humans have for examining the source of those anxieties and other debilitating emotions is called metacognition. What that means is that we can observe who we are being in order to modify our current behavior. We can use our conscious neocortex brain in full awareness to cause the limbic brain or seat of our emotions to produce new neuropeptides and, with repetition, the cerebellum or third brain will register a new subconscious memory replacing the old way of being.

We can re-pattern our memories so that anxiety is replaced by the emotion of love.

Looking back on my life, a curious pattern can be identified. Exciting, life-changing events simply appeared, not by means of my doing. How can that be? On those occasions, I was not actively forcing events in order to express my little will. I was subconsciously allowing my divine will to attract exactly what I really needed within the multi-dimensional field of all possibilities in alignment with the will of the One Consciousness.

The time is indeed now for us to switch from being passive and allowing our subconscious to be in control, to taking the driver's seat with conscious awareness of the choices we, as divine humans, make in our lives. We are divine and an individual expression of the One

Consciousness, but we have forgotten. How would fear of the future shift if we assumed this new role on our journey on the spiral of life? Force no longer would be our means of controlling future events. We would relax into a knowing that magnetism and attraction would bring about a constant flow of synchronicity in our life providing us with the next most perfect adventure to nourish our soul's growth. Shifting into the now is not easy, as the story of my nighttime tossing and turning will show.

My story begins in January of 2012 when I accepted my "contract" to express in the physical what had up to then only been a concept, the S.T.A.R. clinic. The S.T.A.R. clinic had been anchored by me in 2007 and was well-documented in my first book, *Return of Love to Planet Earth: Memoir of a Reluctant Visionary.* The seeds for the physical manifestation of the S.T.A.R. clinic had been planted then and were about to germinate. I was to be not only the anchor but the nurturer for what had never been expressed on planet earth. At the time, the definition of the S.T.A.R. clinic was: a multi-dimensional tool gifted to humanity, by inter-dimensional/inter-galactic forces of great conscious awareness and wisdom, to assist in one's inner alchemy transformation, in preparation for the dimensional shift or ascension.

Just how does one bring into being something that has never been on the planet before? How does one even speak about what has never been on the planet before? In our third-dimensional linear vocabulary, there are no words for the new concepts and constructs that are and will be appearing or will be remembered.

I am encouraged when I reflect on the Dogon tribe, a remote West African people whose current rituals and traditions are known to date from a period as early as 3000 BCE. The Dogon don't base their inner wisdom on current belief systems or even science. They simply know. The tribe continues to use spoken words and symbols instead of a written language to describe things for which they have no scientific proof, according to Laird Scranton, who wrote the book, *Sacred Symbols of the Dogon: The Key to Advanced Science in the Ancient Egyptian Hieroglyphs*.

The Dogon were trying to describe with their hieroglyphs things that they had no language for, or if they did, were not understood by others. We are moving into that place too of attempting to convey new thoughts, which come from our innate knowing but have no logical, linear nor scientific proof.

How am I to describe and express something like the S.T.A.R. clinic? Certainly this is an appropriate example of "fear of the future." Will I be successful in manifesting what has not been on the planet before? Who will attend, since no one knows what the S.T.A.R. clinic is? Who is to be involved? The questions were bombarding my thinking brain and causing me enormous anxiety in the middle of the night. One physical sign of fear, perspiration, was making sleep no longer possible. I was being showered with debilitating emotions and their corresponding neuropeptides! Then I asked the question, "Who is the one who is afraid?" It had to be my ego/personality that was luxuriating in this chemical soup I was generating. How to get out before drowning was what I asked myself.

My thoughts moved to a book I was reading, *The Quantum Doctor*, by Dr. Goswami, and I began to apply some of his methods. I moved all the thoughts that were filling my brain, to my sacred heart. From that space, an intention was created: "The successful outcome of the S.T.A.R. clinic." No details were included in my intention. There was a knowing that, as I surrendered this request to my divinity in alignment with the will of the divine Creator, the details already existed in the multi-dimensional field of all possibilities. I completely let go of the fear that had controlled my emotions during the early hours of the morning.

What I had done was trusted that my intention was expressed within the transcendent field of One Consciousness. I was allowing the waves of possibility, created by the energy of my thoughts, to expand outside of my frame of reference, or the limiting box of my experience, into the

> The perfect outcome exists and awaits the perfect moment to be revealed.

unknown, where they would be collapsed into particle form by my divine will. The outcome or chosen possibility already existed and through appreciation and gratitude would be revealed to me at exactly the perfect moment. How beautiful to resolve the anxiety I had felt about the S.T.A.R. clinic by means of the S.T.A.R. philosophy. I had moved out of the illusional future and into the now, the only moment that truly exists.

The S.T.A.R. clinic has been imagined and has had two expressions in the physical to date. It is beginning to be understood and appreciated by many across the planet, who know it to be a gift to the conscious awakening of humankind to the knowing of human divinity and sovereignty.

S.T.A.R. is how I live my life. There is a deep knowing that all is perfection, even those moments of seeming chaos. On a conscious or subconscious level I AM the creator of my existence. All I need do is choose to surrender, trust, allow and receive. What I receive is always the perfect path for me to take at that precise moment on my journey in order for me to move in conscious awareness on the spiral of life. I am a magician creating my reality, and it is splendid at every moment.

CHOOSING THE UNKNOWN

If we have never experienced the new way of being on earth, how do we know how to create it when the experience is outside of our frame of reference? How do we create something that we have never known? Where do we find the building blocks? The answer is that we, the personality, can't but the divine human can indeed create the unknown, and again we will turn to quantum physics and look at the quantum leap.

Dr. Goswami tells us, "A quantum object ceases to exist here and simultaneously appears in existence over there; we cannot say it went through the intervening space."[26] That is a quantum leap, when an electron does not travel through space, but simply appears somewhere else.

Are we talking about magic? How can a quantum leap be our truth? Well the world of quantum physics is just that—it just is. The determining factor is the observer and, according to Dr. Goswami, the One Consciousness behind the observer, you and You, or the I behind the eye. The You is your human divinity or You as an individual aspect of All That Is. If we believe that we can create the new earth, we have to be speaking of "we" as the "We" that is All That Is. Then and only then can we/We create the new or choose the unknown.

When we choose the unknown, we are choosing from possibilities, not from determined conditions. With a quantum leap, the electron jumps and it is impossible to predict the destination.

"We cannot tell when a particular electron is going to jump nor where it is going to jump if it has more than one lower rung from which to choose. We can only give probabilities."[27]

---

26.   Amit Goswami, PhD, *The Self-Aware Universe: How Consciousness Creates the Material World* (New York, NY: Tarcher/Putnam, 1993), p. 9.

27.   Ibid., p. 30.

So, if we cannot predict where the electron will jump during a quantum leap, perhaps that suggests that when we place an intention into the field, the outcome is not to be predicted but trusted and allowed. Creating the unknown is quantum physics in action: S.T.A.R.

Another principle in the new physics is the wave pattern of possibility, which is the cornerstone of quantum physics, and that it is the observer that chooses the collapse of the wave which creates our reality.

When we surrender and allow the wave of energy to travel outside of our box of known reality and trust our divinity (the One Consciousness) to collapse the wave into its particle state, then we receive the manifestation of the unknown. This, however, can only occur when we know our wholeness, our human divinity.

We, the divine human, can choose from unlimited possibility to create the unknown.

We, the divine human, are connected to the non-local One Consciousness, from which ultimately comes all choice.

Can we make the following deduction: we can choose a new earth from the wave of all possibilities, which when we observe it may leap into its new particle expression? Could it be as simple as that? Is it simply a matter of our knowing who we are that we can do that? S.T.A.R. is the tool we have been gifted to assist us in this simple, but not easy choice of choosing the unknown. Once we have chosen, then we are to take action.

Now Play While You Take Action

When the inner voice speaks, like a compass, it can point us in a different direction than we had expected. The natural response is fear of the unknown and the resulting action is no action. We choose to continue the comfortable behavior that is familiar. The neurotransmitters are shouting out, "Keep the status quo to which the body has become accustomed." So how do we get out of this loop?

Our inner voice is our intuition or our innate knowing, which is a response to our will aligning with the will of the divine Creator or divine wisdom. When our will is in opposition to the patterned behavior of the body, we can unlock the circuits that are "calling the shots" by playing in no time/no space. As Dr. Dispenza suggests, alpha or meditative state disconnects us from body, environment and time. In that space, we can dream about the message we are receiving from our intuition without subconscious interference.

What would these dreams look like and feel like? As we dream, we begin to change the conditioned chemistry and circuits to new chemistry and circuits, and we change our behavior from fear to the emotion of love. From this alpha or theta brain wave state, the conscious and subconscious are flowing together and new thoughts appear or are unlocked. Now our mind and body are correlated, and we are changing our identity and personality to reflect the will of the divine, which is in alignment with our will.

New behavior is now possible, fear has been released and different action is now being chosen, whereas before, the addiction of patterned behavior was blocking us. Now S.T.A.R. is engaged. We have surrendered to the unknown, trusting that our human divinity will guide us, allowing magic to leap into our lives, and we will receive all as a gift from the divine

Creator, whose will we intend to express with gratitude and appreciation.

Now that we have created a new state of being, it is time to take action, to play in the now moment. Action requires discernment. Again within the quantum field of now, we ask the question, "Does this action step reflect an aligned will with the will of the divine?" Then we listen to the innate within for the answer, which is detached from the past or the future.

Play + Discernment will help us to act in alignment with the quantum field of possibilities.

Let me share another personal story about how just taking action caused the multi-dimensional field to respond. Gather Insight, in the person of Ja-lene Clark, approached me to write a book about S.T.A.R. This had not been my idea, so it popped out of the air presenting itself as a total unknown to me (the divine will was speaking). My thought was that any book on this topic would be very short and to the point, so I accepted. Writing occurred when thoughts appeared. Then I was encouraged to expand the book, so I developed a discipline or an action plan for writing a specific amount of text daily. The dilemma I faced was how and where to find the content for a longer book?

Each day, a chapter title appeared. During lucid dream state, my focus would be centered on that day's particular title. There was always a pen and paper by the bed at night so that as ideas popped into my mind, I could write them down. In the morning without looking at the large piece of paper filled with words, I could not easily recall what had been written. What I observed was that the flow of thoughts was dramatically increased when I created my action plan.

The specifics of the plan were:

1. Identify a topic each day;

2. Surrender the topic into no time/no space;

3. Trust that my human divinity would "do the work."

4. Allow the flow of ideas to express through me like a spigot. I received these insights every few minutes in my lucid dreams. When I got in and out of bed for about an hour a night, I expressed appreciation and gratitude for what my will and the divine will had dreamed during the night. Truly, nighttime was my playground!

5. Receive during the day, words that I would hear, a movie that I might watch or books that presented themselves became clues for me to explore to find the specific wisdom that I was to use as a springboard for content or the next daily title.

The most amazing thing was that since the creation process occurred primarily in the alpha state, my brain circuits have been rewiring so that I am living and becoming the content of the book. The book is changing because of me, and I am changing because of this book. My sovereignty is writing my book and authoring my reality. Fascinating!

Just as I have described the creative process used to write this book, so too can this process be used to create a business or to solve a problem. The thoughts that flow are powerful messages of the One Consciousness expressing through us when we are in the octaves of S.T.A.R. Once they are received, accept them with love by taking an action step with the new behavior that is emerging in the new identify of self. As the new personality emerges from one's inner reality, it is reflected in the outer reality and impacts the energy within the field of All That Is. We then are dreaming and manifesting the Golden Age of Divine Love.

Becoming a Now Being

Like your life, mine has been filled with suffering, joy, pain, peace, fear, rapture, uncertainty, courage, trepidation and all the emotions of living on planet earth in duality. I thought it would be interesting to take a peek at one of my experiences, which I lived through before I learned about S.T.A.R. What would it look like if I were to go through it again knowing this time that I am a divine human living in the now? The experience I chose occurred the first few years after I arrived in Santa Fe, New Mexico.

Before I begin, I would like to say that it involves another person, whom I will refer to as Ed. Please know that in no way do I wish to present him, his decisions or his actions as wrong. On the contrary, I wish to acknowledge him as a being of light who participated in the game of life gifting me with a life lesson. Ed is no longer on the planet, so perhaps he is watching me write with amusement saying, "Ah, that is why we made those choices, so that Nina could write about them in her second book."

In 1999, I sold my house in the Philadelphia suburbs in order to pay off debts. I was newly divorced and found myself for the first time in my life trying to make a living. With no experience in the workforce, the jobs that I was qualified for and often a finalist for never came my way because I had no experience. As an alternative to getting a job, I had been advised to start a company, one assisting women business owners with access to capital, and I soon became a nationally recognized expert. What no one knew except my family and good friends was that I was spending capital to build my vision. When I tried to raise money for a venture fund, I was again asked, "Have you done this before?" A good question from someone who was considering investing a great deal of money. To keep the vision alive, I sold the business to a woman venture capitalist and retained an equity position in the company. She was talented and enthusiastic, but did not succeed in raising capital for the fund, so my interest in the project had zero value.

Selling my house gave me enough money to pay off my debts with a little cushion to use to move to Santa Fe, to get an apartment and to begin a new phase of my life. Pre-Paid Legal Services (now called Legal Shield), a multi-level marketing company, was the potential income producing tool that I took with me to New Mexico. I had passion and the market for legal insurance was open, so I felt confident that I would succeed. I joined the Chamber of Commerce almost as soon as I arrived in Santa Fe, so that I could mingle with potential customers.

I met Ed at my first chamber meeting. I remember him standing up in a gathering of about thirty chamber members. He spoke with power and caught my attention. He had a chiseled face with long, dark hair that was tied in a ponytail. His body was mid-height and a bit too thin. He was talking about the indigenous people, who in New Mexico preferred to be called Indians, which also caught my attention. It had occurred to me that the Indian population, as sovereign people, could benefit from the services of Pre-Paid Legal when they interacted off tribal lands. I had wondered how I was going to make contact with a decision-maker, especially not knowing Pueblo culture and council governance. I thought perhaps Ed would be a valuable contact for me to know.

At the end of the meeting, I approached Ed and the saga began. He suggested that we meet to discuss my interest further. He continued to speak with authority about topics that intrigued me. With each breath he was drawing me into his world. There was no resistance from me, only interest, curiosity and a feeling that I would find an answer to how I was going to make a living in Santa Fe.

Ed expanded our conversation away from legal insurance by telling me that he had a pending contract with the government, which would involve the Pueblos in construction contracts. Wow, I had been working with women-owned businesses, now I thought how I would love to work with the Pueblo people in expanding their economic opportunities! I was becoming more excited about new possibilities with each sentence spoken. I began contributing what I could to move this vision forward in the form of money and effort, while Ed was waiting for the contract to be signed.

I arranged a meeting with officials at Los Alamos National Laboratory, whom I had met, and tribal members of Jemez Pueblo, who were friends of new friends I had made. We met to explore the possibility of the lab buying lumber from the native tribe for the lab's construction projects. Everyone was excited and in agreement that a project between the government and the Pueblo people would be a win-win. We were all waiting for Ed's contract to be signed. I was feeling proud having introduced Ed to both the lab and Pueblo council member officials. Perhaps I could have noticed that this was a clue that something was out of balance. How come I had been the one to be the intermediary for the tribe, not Ed, the "Indian" whom I originally had thought was well-connected with council elders.

While all of this was transpiring, my bank account was shrinking. "Any day now," said Ed. My rented furniture was repossessed as my next month's rent was coming due. I can't remember who it was that told me that Ed was not a tribal member, and that he was not any of the things that he had told me he was. There was no pending contract. None of the visits to tribal council meetings had taken place. Nothing had been true. I had spent months in supporting his dream. Every emotion you might imagine was being expressed throughout my body: a sense of failure, heartbreak, disappointment, anger, shock and fear.

To end this story and begin to look at how I would live it today, I want to share with you that a temp agency quickly placed me at Los Alamos Medical Center as the executive assistant to the CEO, where I

Try this: Use a situation that in the past caused you grief. Imagine how using S.T.A.R. might have changed the experience.

worked for the next five years. During that time, the hospital healed me. A daily routine and a paycheck were my medicine. Back taxes were paid over time and an affordable casita became available for me to move in to. Ed disappeared.

Now that the grace of the S.T.A.R. philosophy is how I create and live my experiences, let's go back to the first meeting I attended of the Santa Fe Chamber of Commerce, in the year 2000, and imagine it expressed as I might do so today.

In this new scenario, I have only been in Santa Fe a few months. My life experiences are being lived in the moment, which allows new dimensions of consciousness to open up and coincidences to happen. Pre-Paid Legal Services has presented itself in my life and the company recognizes me as a valuable member of their team. I have money in the bank from the recent sale of my house in the Philadelphia suburbs. I am enthusiastic about my vision to share affordable legal services with the Pueblo people of New Mexico, a market about which I know very little.

A dynamic man, Ed, stands up and speaks powerfully about the issues of the Indians in New Mexico. I am fascinated and listen carefully to each word, hoping to learn. Then it is my turn to present. All the passion that had courageously brought me to Santa Fe begins to pour out of me. I speak to the group about my interest in making affordable legal services available to the sovereign people living in the Pueblos throughout New Mexico. By observing the faces of many in the audience, I feel that my point is being efficiently presented. The chamber members are engaged.

At the end of the meeting, I am approached by someone sitting behind me. He tells me that he is the brother of the current governor of San Ildefonso Pueblo[28] (its traditional name, Po-woh-ge-oweenge, means "where the water cuts through"), and that he would like very much to speak on my behalf to his brother to request that I be invited to introduce our product for consideration by the tribal council elders. He tells me that San Ildefonso Pueblo is a member of the Eight Northern Pueblos Council and that his brother is the chairman of that council. He continues to share that, as chairman of the Eight Northern Pueblos Council (Nambé, Pojoaque, Taos, Tesuque, Picuris, San Ildefonso, Santa Clara and San Juan), his brother might also be able to introduce me to the Indian Pueblo Cultural Center in Albuquerque, in which all nineteen Pueblos in New Mexico are members (additional members: Acoma, Cochiti, Jemez, Isleta, Laguna, Sandia, San Felipe, Santa Ana, Santa Clara, Santo Domingo and Zia). I accept the stranger's invitation with gratitude and appreciation.

How had my actions differed between the actual and the imagined? When I approached Ed twelve years ago, I gave my power away. I was trying to control the events in my life by doing the very best that I could. In the imagined scenario, I had a knowing that my divine wisdom would support me in mystical magical ways. All that I need do was surrender to my divine self, trust that through my intention, the field would express exactly what was perfect for me in each precise moment and through that expression my soul would evolve on the spiral of life. All of this to be received with appreciation and gratitude. I let go and allowed the absolute flow of now to carry me with ease and grace.

---

28. This is not factual, purely the imagination of the author.

I know that the possibility of the imagined scenario could easily have been my reality, for I am experiencing life in exactly that way. While recently being engaged in an enormous project at the Stardreaming site, I had two people say to me, "What do you need?" Both of them approached me with an interest in fully funding our project. I had not asked for anything, merely told them what I was working on. Coincidences happen so often that they are no longer coincidences. The power behind living in the moment fills me with the tranquility of knowing myself as a divine human, from which belief my experiences flow with ease and grace.

Eckhart Tolle tells us, "When you yield internally, when you surrender, a new dimension of consciousness opens up. If action is possible or necessary, your action will be in alignment with the whole and supported by creative intelligence, the unconditioned consciousness which in a state of inner openness you become one with. Circumstances and people then become helpful, cooperative. Coincidences happen. If no action is possible, you rest in the peace and inner stillness that come with surrender. You rest in God."[29]

Dream with me how moving into S.T.A.R. might have attracted a different outcome.

What situations in your life can be rewritten? Think of one situation that has created much angst in your heart. Have you made a

---

29. Eckhart Tolle, *The New Earth: Awakening to Your Life's Purpose* (New York, NY: Penguin Group, 2005), p. 58.

decision based on the influence of another person? Perhaps it was a life choice that took you in a direction that was not in alignment with your soul's desire.

How can you adapt what you learn from this exercise to apply it to the next time you are given a choice? How might the outcome shift when your will is aligned with the will of the divine Creator, and you believe that you are worthy to choose from your innate knowing?

I AM WORTHY

To answer the question "Where do our thoughts come from?" requires that first we answer the question that I believe is the one primary question to be asked, "Who am I?" If you answer Jane or Bob, then the thoughts come from the ego/personality self that is swimming with chemicals defining identity with emotions such as anger, fear, shame. All of these emotions are controlling our thoughts and defining our personality, our behavior and our self-worth.

"I am unworthy to receive" is a thought that comes from the ego/ personality. "I can't do that. I am afraid I might fail. He didn't call me because I am too fat. She turned me down because I have an old car." We can go on and on listening to the thoughts to which our body has become addicted. These thoughts produce survival-oriented emotions that our body has become accustomed to and now requires more and more of, thus urging our mind to keep the dysfunctional thoughts coming. The brain has fired so many times in this pattern that the circuits are now wired.

"The moment we begin to deny ourselves the substance we are addicted to—in this case, the familiar thoughts and feelings associated with our emotional addiction—there are cravings, withdrawal pains, and a host of inner subvocalizations urging us not to change. And so we remain chained to our familiar reality."[30]

When we begin to live into our new identity as a divine human and know ourselves to be worthy, these low-frequency thoughts and resulting feelings no longer serve us. Our goal is to restrain the ego/personality. "When the ego is in check, its natural job is to make sure we are protected and safe in the outer world. As an example, the ego makes sure we stay far away from a bonfire or a few steps away from the cliff's edge."[31]

Changing our thoughts is an inner alchemy process that requires intention and self-observation. How do we break the habit of thinking we are less than perfection? As Dr. Dispenza suggests, this work cannot be done in the environment, body or time in which the negative thoughts were created. We must move into no time/no space to shift octaves.

> Surrender opens our imagination to dream new dreams.

Lucid dream state, alpha brain wave meditation and heart-centered thinking are all ways that we can move out of our attachment to who we have believed we are. Surrendering our attachments is the task that will take us to the zero point where we can dream and imagine what it would feel like to be and live that dream. With repetition, our body begins to fire differently, causing brain circuits to wire differently.

When we identify self with the divine Creator, the pristine octave of emotions within us escalates to the level of love, influences our thoughts

---

30. Dr. Joe Dispenza, *Breaking the Habit of Being Yourself: How to Lose Your Mind and Create a New One* (Carlsbad, CA: Hay House, Inc., 2012), p. 104.

31. Ibid., p. 105.

and a new pattern or way of being is created. This new way of being is reflected from the inner self to the field outside of self, influencing our reality. When we identify with the divine, this moves us into advanced states of trust, where we can make our choices and decisions well beyond the influence of our basic survival thoughts.

Another source where thoughts come from are our cosmic guides or what some people call them, our guiding angels. Once we have tapped into the transcendent field of All That Is, an expanded awareness of creation might appear, and one might develop the gift of being clairaudient, hearing inner voices, which claim to come from a unique identity outside of self. The messages that are received can become a source for one's own thoughts. At first, the amazement of "hearing voices" may dazzle and influence the listener. The question must be asked, "Are the voices clearly sourced from the will of the divine Creator?" One can determine this to be so by holding the intention that "only those voices which express the will of the divine Creator with crystalline clarity be allowed to present." Just as the personality can influence thought in a troublesome manner, so can influence from beings that masquerade as angels. Clarity, discernment and the intention to align one's will with the will of the divine Creator are the means by which the absolutely crystalline flow of thought can be received. You will know without a doubt because there will be an inner wisdom from which will evolve expanded experiences, feelings and influences on behavior.

With integrity, we can intend that our personality step aside and allow the divine within to bring forth the thoughts or information we need at the most appropriate time. These messages increase a sense of peacefulness and validation of who we are as divine humans. Imagining that we are worthy to receive this inner wisdom comes in when we apply the S.T.A.R. philosophy.

Repatterning Our Response System

Am I who I appear to be, or do I appear as I believe the environment wants me to show up? Do I crave attention and validation from others for being a specific way? Am I truly letting my soul be seen? Am I transparent and appearing as who I really am, a divine human? There are so many controlling factors surrounding us to feed our habitual emotions. When those emotions are fed, we become addicted to the feeling and lock into a subconscious pattern of being. Our body requires our patterned behavior to amplify in order to cause the limbic brain to produce greater and greater quantities of the same chemicals, neuropeptides, to satisfy the cell receptor sites which are becoming immune and need more stimulation.

"But if receptor sites are continually stimulated, they get desensitized and shut off. So they need a strong signal, a bit more stimulation, to turn them on the next time—it takes a bigger chemical high to produce the same effects."[32]

> It is a gift and opportunity to rise to another octave when family or loved ones push our buttons.

If we wish to live in the now and by S.T.A.R., how do we look at the shadow side of our personality in order to identify the habitual emotions that are causing a behavior that we now feel does not define us? So often I have heard people say, "I just can't stay in the now. When I am at family reunions, all of my buttons are pushed and I slip out of it."

The process begins by going gently and deeply within through self-observation and metacognition and looking at life's experiences to identify patterns and ways of being caused by an emotional charge. All

---

32. Ibid., p. 168.

thoughts, feelings and their resulting behavior are to be examined from this life and perhaps going even deeper, from past lives.

When the emotions are identified, such as fear, insecurity, anger, shame, self-doubt and guilt, we can then move into a meditative state to work with them. Each experience in our life has an emotion attached to it. As an example, in meditation you might ask, "What would it look like to not feel fear when I am in the presence of Sally? How would it feel to not have fear when I am in the presence of Sally?" Then, imagine and feel this new way of behaving. What you are doing is releasing the emotion of fear in this situation into the now. It is losing its charge or control. You are moving into a higher frequency of emotion, such as joy. When you next meet Sally, the neural wiring will have been disconnected, and you will have created new circuits causing new feelings and behavior. You will be appearing in a new way.

My friend was planning a dinner to celebrate her daughter's thirtieth birthday. Her daughter wanted homemade lasagna. She went shopping and got all the food to make this dish. She bought her daughter a special cake from the best bakery in her town. She shared that after she had finished her shopping, that her daughter called and wanted her to also make her special recipe for asparagus for the party. When she went shopping for the asparagus, the price had shot up to $5 a pound. She would need three pounds to make enough for everyone. With me she shared, "My primal reaction was to say that is too expensive and we can't afford it. What happened is that I shot back in time to when my daughter was little and money was tight. I found myself triggered into this old thought pattern...'must manage money so I can feed the kids.' 'Must sacrifice my needs to provide for the children.' Because of my work with S.T.A.R., I had the awareness to notice and observe my reactions and to say to myself that now we CAN afford that and even if we couldn't, I was doing it anyway! This awareness occurred at the grocery store. If my daughter wants asparagus, by golly we will have plenty for everyone! I have noticed this tendency in myself to revert back in time when interacting with my kids. That self-awareness has been so freeing. Now I am consciously choosing how to deal with each and every situation."

By choice, we can identify a state of lack, want, anger, or fear and move our conscious awareness into the neutral field of now, from which we can dream a new experience and attract those chosen possibilities to ourselves to express our new imagined reality. The creative energy that we have habitually used in the expression of the debilitating, patterned emotions will be released into the quantum field, since energy cannot be destroyed. It will then be available to

How to change the world:

Shift so that others may shift, while knowing that when others shift, those they are interacting with also shift...and on and on...

return in the new creative energy of joy and love. In the example given earlier, our observation and reaction to our friend Sally then shifts, the emotional bond that she had toward us also must shift, thus impacting the future relationship we both will experience.

This principle of being self-aware can be applied to all the aspects of your life once clearly identified. What is your relationship with money? Why are you feeling unfulfilled in your job? Go to the core emotion and identify it. That awareness can blossom in a fraction of a second just like it did with my friend in the grocery store. Very often the emotion is related to self-worth. Are you in a relationship because it validates how you are appearing to those around you—poor me, my husband doesn't treat me well. Deep within, most likely you do not practice loving yourself. Identify that inner quality, and turn it around consciously. "What would it look like if I loved and respected myself? How would I be and feel when my husband interrupts me when I talk or he doesn't listen to me?" By imagining the answer, you become the answer. You change the wiring and allow love in. The energy of that love permeates your field and shifts, to some degree, your relationship with your husband, who might have felt an energy of neediness or hostility being projected from you, which caused him to disengage.

You are in control once you begin "doing the work." You can consciously change your thoughts, feelings and behavior to reflect who you are. You can stop being who you are because of what you believe the world is expecting or the way you have become because of habit.

We use the phrase, "remove the blocks," to describe other forms of "doing the work." These blocks are memory patterns that are stored at the cellular level. All memory is encoded at the cellular level. The Nobel Prize winner Ivan Petrovich Pavlov, a Russian physiologist, spent thirty years studying brain function and "conditioned reflex." He concluded the conditioned reflex was associated with memory.[33] Stevan Thayer, creator of Integrated Energy Therapy stated, "Every cell in our body has the ability to remember."[34]

Cellular memory implies that consciousness exists in the molecules of our nervous system. As Bruce H. Lipton, PhD, explains, "By extension, it is also perceived by a majority of scientists that the human mind and consciousness are 'encoded' in the molecules of the nervous system. This in turn promotes the concept that the emergence of consciousness

---

33. Thomas R. McClaskey, DC, CHT, BCETS, "Decoding Traumatic Memory Patterns at the Cellular Level," The American Academy of Experts in Traumatic Stress, www.aaets.org/index.html.

34. Stevan Thayer, "Cellular Memory Cell Level Healing," Phoenix and Leon, www.spiritofmaat.com/sep07/cellular_memory.html.

reflects the 'ghost in the machine.'"[35] "Doing the work" then would suggest that negative memory is to be removed or changed at the cellular level.

We now know that the body doesn't know the difference between the actual experience and a memory of an experience. We can, and I have, dreamed alternative experiences, which have become new memories for me. They are now just as "real" as an actual experience is. In other words, I can rewrite my past. Can we not rewrite cellular memory in the same way?

The neocortex (the brain's frontal lobe) is where thought occurs. The limbic brain is the emotional center, and the cerebellum is the location for non-declarative memories. If as suggested earlier, the human mind (thought, emotion & memory) and consciousness are encoded in the molecules of the nervous system, then one can deduce that this encoding can be changed as well.

So once we identify in the molecules of the nervous system the location of a wounded memory, we can consciously change that negative memory to one that is positive. It is possible, and we must do the important inner alchemy work to identify and remove energy blocks. This "work" raises one's frequency to that of love.

To give an example of changing cellular memory, I am going to make an assumption that past-life memory is also stored in the cells. In doing my personal inner alchemy work, I communicated with the consciousness of my cells and asked that areas that were holding a memory wound would be identified. Over a period of a week, I noticed that my right

---

35. Bruce H. Lipton, PhD, "Insight into Cellular Consciousness," posted on 05/08/07 and filed under *Uncovering the Biology of Belief*. Reprinted from Bridges, 2001 Vol 12(1):5 ISSEEM, www.brucelipton.com/biology-of-belief/insight-into-cellular-consciousness.

elbow was very tender when it came into contact with any surface. At first I went through self-diagnosis, "Is it bruised...?" and then I remembered the intention I had placed in the multi-dimensional field.

In lucid dream state, a past-life memory appeared. In the memory, I was a male, dressed in a suit of armor, holding a lance in my right hand. My opponent was also in a suit of armor. An inner knowing came to me that he was my brother in that past lifetime. The pain in my elbow came from the stored memory of the impact that the tip of my lance had made when I had successfully killed my brother. I asked my body to feel the pain of this event. Then my memory switched and the lance became a sword, then a gun and then even a sling shot. Apparently, I was remembering lives when I was a warrior and had killed.

I then asked myself, "How would I experience each event today, knowing what I know and living the S.T.A.R. philosophy?" An answer appeared when I remembered what I had recently learned. When we let society dictate what our behavior will be at anytime, and it is out of alignment with our inner guidance, we will feel pain and suffering. As shared by Abraham-Hicks, an example would be: to be in the military and to follow the rules and even to kill is not the source of suffering. The pain comes from pleasing others and defying who we truly are as divine humans.[36] So the answer to my recalled past-life events and the way to remove their cellular memory wound was to change the memory of being out of integrity with the core of my being. I, therefore, went deep within and created a situation that was coherent with my internal vibration: putting the lance down and negotiating.

Inner alchemy is "doing the work," and it is critical to achieving the emotional vibration of love, from which we manifest our new external

---

36. Abraham-Hicks: "War, Pets and Alignment,"
www.lawofattractioninteraction.com/war-pets-alignment.php.

reality. This is a key for creating the new earth, the Golden Age of Divine Love.

WILLINGLY TAKING DIRECTION FROM OUR OWN DIVINE SELF—A NEW LEVEL OF CONFIDENCE

We have spent years following the spiritual direction of others, looking outside of ourselves for guidance in matters of the spirit. The idea that our divine wisdom lies within is new for many and for me as well. How can we trust this remembering? It is indeed a remembering, for there was a time when we knew this to be true. I believe that during the Golden Age of Lemuria and the Golden Age of Atlantis we knew our divinity. Then we forgot. How do we return to a sovereign state of being? The personality tries to block us by screaming "Pride! Arrogance! Be humble? Not you!" Yet within, there is a yearning to surrender, trust and allow this possibility to expand and to then receive fully the love of you for YOU.

As we open this door of a new reality and walk in as the master that we are, the devil and the angel sitting on our shoulders will be trying to get our attention. One way to merge the polarities tugging at us in opposite directions and to achieve self-realization is by means of community. Seek with intention those beings of light on the planet who radiate the harmonics of the divine Creator. Sit by their side. Listen to their words and entrain with their frequency. You will unlock the veiled memory of your truth and, with each clear breath of life filling your Being, will awaken to the knowing in every cell, that you are a divine human. The community of sovereign beings will support you in transitioning to your wholeness until you can stand tall and be a model for others.

When you seek answers to the many questions that will arise on this journey of self-realization, look within to your own quantum field, the energetic you that is not expressed in the physical. The answers are within the consciousness of your field. You need merely have the intention and the field will provide the answers, but you must *ask* for the inner wisdom to be revealed. The innate, intuitive knowing that is your inner compass will guide you. Trusting this to be your truth will perhaps begin slowly as you explore working with your field. The divine wisdom it contains will reveal itself to you as you allow it to.

The challenge to regaining the remembering of your human divinity will be the environment that surrounds you. What will my best friend think if I declare that I am an individual aspect of All That Is? Will I be rejected, laughed at or even worse thought to be wrong?

Once again, holding the intention of attracting a community of like-minded beings will support you as you process these experiences. What you will observe is that, as you begin to radiate the energy of this inner knowing, your external reality will begin to shift.

Those around you will experience the frequency of your field and will choose consciously or subconsciously to shift their energetic frequency. However, some people may feel uncomfortable and unable to change, so they will leave. Often the separation of couples and friends is because of a change in one's energy field more than from words spoken or actions taken. We are merely moving on the spiral of life differently than those who choose to separate from us.

"Think of emotions as 'energy in motion.' If you share the same emotions, you share the same energy…you are bonded in an invisible field of energy to every thing, person, and place in your external life.

Bonds between people are the strongest, though, because emotions hold the strongest energy."[37]

When people change emotionally, their bonds to everything in their life change. Marching to a different drummer may be challenging, but in time you will observe that others are awakening to the harmonics of that drum beat, the beat of the sacred heart.

THE FASCINATED OBSERVER

With "fascination" is the most empowered manner in which the observer experiences the soul's journey on the spiral of life. From the vantage point of fascination, one is participating in what is presented—from experiences, to events, to conversations and in relationships, with the delight of watching what shows up. Fascination allows one to ask, "Wow, why did I create that?"

As an observer of one's life, circumstances lose their power to effect negative emotions. My favorite example is when one goes to the supermarket and stands behind a person who has eleven items in the ten-items-only, check-out aisle. The typical reaction is to hold an internal dialogue that goes something like this, "He ought to go back to school and learn how to count!!!!!! I am going to be late for my dog grooming appointment. How could she do this to me?"

The situation is really all about us. Why am I getting so disturbed? Why am I feeling this way? The event, whatever it might be, just is. It is how we react to it that is causing thought, feeling and behavior. A different way to respond, as the observer, to seeing eleven grocery items

---

37. Dr. Joe Dispenza, *Breaking the Habit of Being Yourself: How to Lose Your Mind and Create a New One* (Carlsbad, CA: Hay House, Inc., 2012), pp. 156–157.

in front of you, is to ask, "How is my life going to be different because of this perceived delay?" Could it be that you are still in the store when your best friend enters? Perhaps being put on a different time schedule allowed you to miss a negative event that you would have been involved in had you exited earlier. Or did the quiet time standing in line allow you to have an "Ah-ha!" thought that would not have occurred had you rushed out the door?

To expand on this thought, let me share a personal experience which happened in the Santa Fe post office. The time was about ten o'clock and the line of customers was unusually long. I had one overnight letter to post, so leaving was not an option. The woman two people ahead of me had a shopping cart filled with what seemed like thirty-five boxes. I learned from overhearing her conversation, how she sold her products through eBay, the online shopping and auction network, and this was her second visit to the post office that day.

While I was standing in the line, which turned out to be for a little under an hour, I shifted my mind to the question, "Why am I in such a slow line, just standing here?" Then a thought came to me, "Stand up straight." Curious, I pulled my shoulders back and held a very erect posture. The muscles in my back began to ache, but I held firmly. Then I remembered that I had spent the last week crouched in a sofa watching hours and hours worth of the 2012 Olympic Games being televised from London, England. No wonder my posture was poor. After a half hour, the muscles stopped hurting and it felt natural to stand so straight. What had possibly seemed like a disruption to the flow of my day had turned out to be a gift in disguise.

To be an observer in the octaves of S.T.A.R. removes judgment. The eBay vendor was not wrong. The line of people wishing to use the postal service was not wrong. The event that appeared in my life, just was. One might call this mode of observing a form of innocent perception: to be aware without bias.

Glenda Green writes, "Through innocent perception, you may also perceive the presence of God in all of existence. This is purity of perception."[38]

For example, when we meet a person who has on a black leather jacket, it is easy to assume that they are a motorcycle rider. Innocent perception allows us to merely observe that the jacket is black and leather, without assigning a quality, characteristic and behavior to the person choosing to wear the jacket. We are merely allowing the identity or personality of the individual to unfold. We know that, under all the signs and symbols, we might observe that the true identity of the person that we have just met is an individual aspect of All That Is expressing and experiencing in a unique way.

Another way to be an observer is to be aware of our bodies. How do the environment and time cause emotional responses? When we notice how thoughts make us feel, then we are able to reflect on the thoughts and make a different choice if signs of discomfort are present. While daydreaming, I

NOTICE
how your thoughts make
you FEEL.

had a thought about a project I was involved in. I noticed that my body tightened up as I projected that thought into the future. I was noticing my physical response to the emotion of fear. I took my thought out of future time and moved it into my sacred heart, the now, and the feeling disappeared. I chose to dream about the event and to see it occurring in a manner that gave me delight. My feelings shifted to a calm sense of

---

38. Glenda Green, *Love Without End: Jesus Speaks* (Sedona, AZ: Spiritis Publishing, 1999), p. 234.

joy. I saw myself and all the participants involved in the project. All was unfolding beautifully. Then I asked the question: "Is there an action step for me to take to facilitate the successful outcome of my dream?" The answer was: "Let go. Surrender, trust, allow and receive what it is that you have imagined with appreciation and gratitude." My will was aligned with the will of the divine Creator. The event would express perfectly.

BECOME THE DIVINE MASTER THAT YOU ALREADY ARE

We, unaware of our human divinity, have been perfection, *walking masters,* seeking the expression of perfection, the will of the divine Creator. As we remember our wholeness, we become perfection, *walking masters,* expressing perfection, the will of the divine Creator. How can it be otherwise when we know ourselves as interconnected with All That Is. This is mastery. This is impeccability. This is the crystalline clear expansion of the One Consciousness in human form. We are already and have always been perfect. We have just forgotten, and this is the grand time of awakening of souls on the planet, the shift in dimensions.

Why do we seek to remember our mastery or human divinity? It is in our quantum DNA field to seek to know our divinity. Lee Carroll explains that Layer Ten, named Vayikra, can also be called "The Divine Source of Existence...This energy is, therefore, one that responds to spiritual intent, questions and puzzles. It is there to assist those who ask, 'Is there really a God? I want to know.' Those who ask it in an academic way will get an academic energy, not the belief layer. This one responds to pure intent and compassion; it simply allows for learning, and still does nothing to teach or convince. Instead, it helps posture grace and understanding, allowing the Human to discover on his own."[39] This is an example of free will gifted to humanity. Do we choose to hold the intention, to know our human divinity, with love or not, in order to achieve mastery?

The process of intentionally returning to the forgotten state of mastery is an inner alchemy transformation or "doing the work." This work cannot be done for us, nor is the experience to be taken away from us. This is why we incarnated, to create experiences that would awaken each of us individually to the knowing of our human divinity.

Holding an intention in the now is a multi-dimensional transformational process to reawaken one's mastery. "I hold the intention that my will be aligned with the will of the divine Creator in all that I think, all that I feel and all that I create to experience." We will become the master and the observer of our reality instead of our external environment being the master of us. With each repetition of

> When your actions and beliefs align, life flows with more grace and ease.

this intention, inner alchemy or new firing and wiring of the brain circuits will occur, raising the frequency of our emotions to that of love, which becomes the new habit of being or a new personality.

In this state of impeccability, we will "walk the talk," by aligning our actions to our beliefs. Life will flow with ease and grace as synchronicity and coincidence appear more and more often as if being gifted by the multi-dimensional field. The opportunities for growth, expansion and transformation are infinite in the transcendent field of all possibilities.

---

39. Lee Carroll, *The Twelve Layers of DNA (An Esoteric Study of the Mastery Within)*, Kryon Book Twelve (Sedona, AZ: Platinum Publishing House, 2010) pp. 190, 191, 192.

Exploring the realm of infinite possibilities is exciting. But, we are alive here on planet earth and so learning how to use S.T.A.R. in everyday life situations is necessary. For me, S.T.A.R. was first an intuitive knowing, a desire to live my life differently. There was initially no name for this feeling. Perhaps my desire attracted James F. Jereb to me so that he could introduce the S.T.A.R. concept. The same yearning may be latent in you as well.

NOW WITH CONTEMPLATION, INQUIRY, EXAMINATION AND WAYS OF APPLICATION HAVING BEEN PRESENTED, YOU HAVE THE RAW MATERIAL FOR BEING ENVELOPED BY THE OCTAVES OF S.T.A.R.

APPLYING THE WISDOM OF S.T.A.R. IN EVERYDAY SITUATIONS

It is one thing to enjoy learning and ideas, yet actually apply-ing that wisdom to real life situations can be challenging. Often after we read, with great exuberance, we journey out into the world and try to apply those philosophies to our life. The ideals of surrender, trust, allow, receive are simple, but applying these in real-world situations takes practice, commitment and diligence. To help you integrate these ideas, in this section we have included explorations showing everyday situations so that you can reflect on applying S.T.A.R. to your life experience.

With peace and inner stillness comes S.T.A.R. wisdom. We are certain we have arrived when we receive a conscious know-ing deep within that has no emotional charge, a state in which the personality self and the divine self are in exquisite balance. Using S.T.A.R. wisdom, knowing that we are sovereign beings, we can ask:

"WHAT WOULD I LIKE TO CREATE AND HOW WOULD I LIKE TO PRESENT AND BE?"

CONSCIOUSLY USING OUR PERSONAL POWER

Personal power is the result of the S.T.A.R. philosophy. Being in the now moment with no attachment to past memories or future fears gives us an inner strength with which to experience seemingly negative events such as abuse. In essence, this means that we are liberated from what has imprisoned us. At first the idea of applying surrender, trust, allow and receive to abusive experiences might sound inappropriate. In no way is this a suggestion that one should surrender to an abuser, trust someone who is harming you, allow any disrespect to you or receive improper treatment. There is a deeper application, which moves one's understanding beyond the third-dimensional view of such an event. Always we must go to the core of all issues and ask the question, "Who am I?" If the answer is "Alice" or "Al," we could have one outcome from an abusive situation. If the answer is "Wholeness," we will have a different outcome or perhaps at that level of conscious awareness, we will not have attracted abuse as a teacher to us at all.

The abuse that I experienced in the early 1990s occurred before I knew myself as a divine human and before I had been introduced to the wisdom of S.T.A.R. The story is poignant; however, it was my intuitive actions and words ending the experience that align so perfectly with S.T.A.R. The story might answer the reader's question, "Nina, how did you achieve this S.T.A.R. wisdom?" The answer is, "I achieved it one experience at a time, and this was one of those pivotal experiences."

Let me start the story by saying that three months ago I received a phone call from a man, whose voice I did not recognized and who also did not give me his name. He must have felt that after almost twenty years I would recognize that it was Norman. After learning who was calling, I observed my body's physical reaction. It was calm. The words that came out of my mouth were calm. I listened carefully. Norman said that he was calling to apologize.

The apology was for abusive behavior that began after I declared that the relationship, both professional and personal, between Norman and me could no longer be sustained. The physiological reasons for Norman's abrupt change in behavior are beyond my understanding, but a guess might be that he experienced a sense of rejection, which he was not willing to accept. The details of his abusive behavior are not relevant other than for me to say that I became paralyzed in his presence and whenever he would try to contact me. My response to Norman's actions was so deeply felt that when I was preparing to sell my house in the Philadelphia suburbs to move to Santa Fe, I tried very hard to keep my destination a secret, so that he would not find me.

I owe my shift in awareness to a stranger from California, with whom I was having an email exchange. How we met, even her name, has drifted from my memory, but her gift will remain with me through-out this lifetime. In one of our emails, I must have shared my current trauma and the impact it was having on me. She asked me a surprising question, "If a two-year-old child does something wrong, would you kick him out of the house?" Of course I wouldn't. "Well, Norman is a very young soul and is to be treated the same way." These few words were life changing for me.

For the first time, I saw Norman as a being of light traveling through the University of Earth experience. I recognized him as a divine human not as his ego/personality self. But how was I to translate that new thought into action? I had a strong desire to take action so, shortly after integrating these new thoughts, I drove down the Schuylkill Expressway, outside of Philadelphia, on my way to Manayunk, when a voice inside of me said, "Continue on the expressway to the office. Do not turn left to go to Manayunk," Too impossible! The office being referenced was the space in south Philadelphia that Norman and I had used to manage our business. He had locked me out of it. Why should I go there? The answer is that I follow my intuitive inner compass. When I arrived at the office, a convenient parking space was available near to the door. The door was unlocked, and as I entered I saw Norman in the back room. I went up to him, looked him deeply in the eyes and said, "I have something to say to you." He followed me to the sofa, where we both sat looking at each other.

Expanded Love has no definition.

"Norman, I want you to know that I love you, and I am so grateful for the experience that we have had together. I do not wish to continue and will go my own way now, but I love you."

The love I was expressing was not a small love; it was the expanded love that has no definition, the love of one divine human for another divine human.

Norman was speechless. What occurred was that he immediately lost the power that I had given to him. Our relationship moved into a balanced one. For me, it was the beginning of a new love affair with me. That was the gift Norman gave to me—an opportunity to learn self-love. This experience was invaluable and propelled me along the spiral of life.

Looking back with a greater awareness of my human divinity, I understand that life is an experience, one which provides each of us an opportunity to choose to expand or not to expand. Norman was not the abusing man that was seemingly disrupting my life. He was an enormous being of light playing a role in an experience that I had chosen to provide me with a life lesson. How could I not love him, a divine human, for that? With my words to Norman, the abuse began to stop and I moved on to another experience, which taught me another life lesson.

S.T.A.R. USE OF PERSONAL POWER

When we have personal power we can:

Surrender the role of victim

Trust in the truth that the other person (perpetrator) was also a divine being

Allow for intuition to guide into a means of reconciliation, so that any abuse stops

Receive a new level of self-love

In this example, each of the Essential Qualities is activated when:

Wholeness (human divinity) is recognized in self and the other beings involved in the situation.

Self-love is practiced when the event is seen from a positive vantage point as an opportunity for growth.

Play (the now moment) occurs through imagining or daydreaming a new ending to a once painful story.

Embodiment of the Expanded Golden Rule is achieved when the "perpetrator" is seen as a divine being.

S.T.A.R. Relationships with All of Creation

In the S.T.A.R. philosophy the most important relationship is with ourselves, which then impacts our relationship with all of creation. Self-love is the bottom of the food chain of love and is, therefore, one of the four foundational pillars. If you do not love yourself, how can you have appropriate empathy for others? You will be seeking love from outside of yourself, thus draining the energy of your relationships in an unbalanced exchange of energy.

S.T.A.R. wisdom knows that the divine *and* the ego/personality will always be involved in our relationship with others. The personality serves as the translator for the divine mind to execute behavior in the physical plane, in balance with the absolute flow of the positive emotion of love. It contributes to the soul's experience on planet earth. When it believes that it is to run the show, then external relationships are manipulated by the will of the personality, which thrives in the realm of lower frequency emotions such as judgment, shame, fear and anger.

Living in wholeness as a divine human, a balanced identity of self is grounded in self-love and no longer needs to feed off the energy of others to fill the void created by low self-esteem. When we are nourished by self-love, and the transcendent dimension is operating in the background, we can observe the state of being of another without being influenced by it or wishing to change it by force. We interact as sovereign beings, when there is no higher authority than one's innate knowing within.

When we transition into the S.T.A.R. philosophy, our energy field or frequency shifts, which impacts relationships.

A friend or a partner may feel uncomfortable being in the new energy we are emitting and choose to leave. The separation is not because of what we have said or done, but merely because of the high vibration of our newly expanded energy field. There is another possible outcome. The friend might wish to entrain and expand their field to become compatible with ours, by means of the law of resonance. This law states that when one vibrating system (physical body) comes into contact with another vibrating system (another physical body), the vibration of the weaker body will adjust its energy to match that of the stronger body. In other words, the vibration of the stronger system will adjust the energy of the weaker system. Our energies are playing in the field that surrounds and connects us.

To nourish our energy field as a sovereign being, we no longer have to turn to another person from whom to draw energy; we now know more fully that we can go out into nature to receive an abundant supply. In nature, we can breathe more deeply the life force that the free air and nature that surrounds us supplies. Another vast source comes from deep within in the stillness of no time/no space and from which we can draw from the multi-dimensional field that merges with us when we consciously connect.

From that inner world, we experience an understanding of the relationships we have established. Family and friends can be observed as a brother or a neighbor, or they can be known as enormous beings of light who have incarnated to play the game of maya (illusion) with us to assist us on our spiral of life and expanded consciousness. Are they truly the alcoholic or abuser they appear to be? Is that their true identity, or are they, as you are, an individual aspect of the One Consciousness? How we perceive them is how we will relate to them. In my truth, the alcoholic relative presented in my life to teach me a life lesson. My interaction was best when it was motivated by love rather than a desire to force a change. Rescuing another from their "perceived unwanted" condition removes their life's experience. They incarnated to "do the work." It is not for me to "make it right." There is a gem in each experience, which is to be discovered by the individual.

Relationships also include people of different cultures, nations and physical appearance. They too are beings of enormous light and part of All That Is. When we each stand tall in the knowing of our own sovereignty, then there will be no need for aggression or control. Power will come from within and not have to be sought by means of land manipulation, subjugation or discrimination. Who are we trying to discriminate against? They are us, and we are them. We just dress and talk differently, for the fun of the experience.

We also have relationships that are embedded in our memories of the past, in the multi-dimensional field of no time/no space. These memories co-exist in the now. They are part of our chemical firing and wiring and can be changed. The body does not know the difference between an experience and a thought, as was mentioned previously. We can change the past. When one enters an alpha or theta state of merging the conscious with the subconscious, we can explore memories and locate patterns of behavior. Then with imagination and repetitive choosing, the brain connections reset to replace the feelings of those experiences with feelings of love. The altered memory becomes "real" and impacts the body, the identity and behavior, thus shifting the past, present and future within the no time of the now.

In the new energy of the now, it is imperative that we adjust our traditional relationships with our elders. The grandmothers and the grandfathers, the elders in a tribe (any community), carry divine wisdom from which others might learn. Divine wisdom expands over time, by means of experience, allowing for S.T.A.R. wisdom to be lived by the older generation. Our ancestors are to be embraced and included, not excluded or rejected. When we move into the now, we will have time to listen to and learn from their stories, to play together in the illusion we are experiencing together.

Our relationship to the children must shift as well. The children who are incarnating are evolutionally advanced and hold a different level of awareness and consciousness. They are conceptual learners who are empathic and many of them have psychic gifts. The traditional environment that surrounds them is linear and dualistic. This is challenging their relationships with their families, educational systems and societies in which they are rarely recognized or understood. Therefore the method of teaching and the parenting skills must adjust to accommodate these conceptual thinkers, who have less tolerance for *the way it is or the way it has always been done*. From these beautiful beings we can expect the question, "Now, tell me again just why do I *have* to hate my neighbor?" to come out of their mouths. They are to be included, just like the elderly and not made to feel different or inferior. We can observe their differences and rejoice, recognizing that their new level of consciousness is of great importance to the awakening of humankind. They will be the planet's agents of change into a new earth, which we are beginning to dream.

> ALL people are beings of enormous light and a precious part of All That Is.

One of our most important relationships is to all of nature, for in the quantum field of discrete energy, they are us as well expressing at a different vibration in particle form. When we take that expanded view of nature, perhaps we will shift our respect for all of creation. We no longer are superior. We have a different frequency and awareness. Our brain can analyze and forecast amongst other gifts that make us different, but not better. Soon, we will be expanding our relationships to include beings from other dimensions and other galaxies. They too are us, and we are them. Welcoming their different appearances, vibrational states and experiences will gift each one of us with knowing other expressions of Source.

We might conclude by asking about our relationship with beings of dark energy. They have to exist within duality. Where there is light there is dark. What is our relationship to "the dark?" The lower vibrational energy forces thriving in the dark can challenge us, but when we are expressing fully in the light, the lower vibrational energy has no power. Dark cannot exist in the light unless we forget and let the light go out.

Balanced relationships occur when one has surrendered to the tranquility of knowing human divinity, trusted in wholeness to express, allowed human divinity to evolve and received with appreciation and gratitude what wholeness has imagined and chosen.

S.T.A.R. RELATIONSHIPS

When we are in divine relationship we can:

Surrender the will to hold onto relationships that no longer serve the greater good of all parties

Trust that each being involved is expressing their own octave of divinity in a manner that is appropriate in the now moment

Allow the quantum field to create new possibilities for wholesome relationships with all of creation

Receive new imaginative ways to interact

In this example, each of the Essential Qualities is activated when:

Wholeness (human divinity) once recognized in self and other beings transforms the relationships.

Self-love creates the opportunity for appropriate empathy.

Play (the now moment) allows the illusion to just be with no power beyond the maya.

Embodiment of the Expanded Golden Rule creates freedom in these relationships and the room for expansive love.

THE DISAPPEARANCE OF FORGIVENESS

When there is no one to blame there is nothing to forgive. The eradication of blame is a necessary leap in consciousness that humanity is called to take. The disappearance of forgiveness can only happen when we move our understanding of reality away from material realism and accept that we are all One Consciousness made up of waves of possibility, not atoms that are solid.

If we are united waves of possibility emanating from consciousness, then what are we forgiving? All we have to forgive is an experience of that consciousness in which we are an integral part. We are playing in the field of all possibilities, choosing experiences for our soul's growth. However, if we step back into our personality (separation), which defines reality as matter, not spirit, then acts of another can wound the personality, thus forgiveness became a powerful management tool that emerged when we judged that we or something was wronged.

How can anything be wrong if all is the creation of individuated aspects of the One Consciousness? All is perfect and just is. As creator beings, we create, and then we experience what it is that we have created whether perceived as negative or positive. It is just an experience—a challenging lesson or opportunity for the expansion of collective consciousness into a greater awareness of the divinity of all.

Forgiveness is a quality of the personality, which dwells in a specific time and space and has structured boundaries. The personality disappears in expanded dimensional awareness of no time and no space. In the moment, we can rewrite our personal dictionaries. Hope could be another word one might delete in our new earth dictionary. As creator beings, we create with divine will, love and wisdom. The personality self is merely the identity that *hopes* that change will occur.

As a divine human, debilitating emotions such as shame, for which one might seek forgiveness, are replaced by the significantly more pleasant frequency emotion of love for self. There is an intuitive knowing that all of our thoughts, feelings and actions come from love. If an action does not come from love, we can discern that it is merely the behavior of an evolving being…nothing to forgive.

When we acknowledge that the events we experience are opportunities for life lessons to be revealed, then we can have love for the person or events gifting us with those opportunities. The person who enters our life presenting themselves as an

> We ARE united waves of possibility playing in fields of possibilities.

alcoholic or abusive is you, is me, is an aspect of All That Is playing a vital role in the expansion of our awareness. They, too, are on the spiral of life seeking consciously or subconsciously the awakening of their human divinity. How they interact with us is always about our growth, not theirs. Could a specific situation be an opportunity to learn self-love? When we would have forgiven another for their actions "against" us, the judgment converts into love of the other for the experience they have provided our soul. One becomes the observer of life more than the player.

Forgiveness disappears when one has surrendered to the tranquility of knowing human divinity, trusted in wholeness to express, allowed human divinity to evolve and received with appreciation and gratitude what wholeness has imagined and chosen.

S.T.A.R. BEYOND FORGIVENESS

When we know that everything just IS we can:

Surrender the need and instinctive desire to blame

Trust that all that is occurring is orchestrated by the inherent divine nature of each being involved

Allow self to observe what is occurring rather than be taken into the chaos of the drama

Receive emancipation from holding the debilitating thoughts

In this example, each of the Essential Qualities is activated when:

Wholeness (human divinity) is recognized in self and the other beings redefining how the events of life are interpreted.

Self-love creates the momentum to express accelerated levels of love to other beings.

Play (the now moment) allows for the soul's growth in the field of all possibilities.

Embodiment of the Expanded Golden Rule eradicates the need for forgiveness.

DRAMA: THE END

Drama has several definitions, including being a play involving conflicting or contrasting characters. The definition of drama relevant to S.T.A.R. wisdom is about how one relates to the world. Being in a state of no drama in this instance suggests equilibrium of emotions, a state in which we no longer overreact to or exaggerate the importance of events. What is, is. The events simply are. Our new wisdom, which has no emotional spark, allows us to be or not to be the observer of events, without identifying with them or getting a chemical "high" from them.

As we usher in the new ways of being on earth, drama will continue to be presented in the news releases chosen by the television networks. Reality shows, which disqualify contestants in a slow process of making the losers less than, evil or wrong, could still be available. Political campaigns will continue to discredit, bash and blame the opponent. Celebrities will be chased by the paparazzi. We may see a car crash on the highway and not resist looking. However, all of these dramatic situations will disappear slowly if demand and/or our interest decreases.

How we choose to be when drama shows up in our life is the issue, not the question: "What can we do to change these events?" Change will occur over time as change occurs within, one person at a time. We are allowing the old way of learning from suffering to diminish and trying out new ways to experience life. Knowing that we are sovereign, divine humans, and that we no longer identify with the external environment as being who we are, we become observers: in the world, but not of it.

We can hold love for those who are the focus of the nightly news (if we choose to watch). Judgment can no longer be generated within us, for we know that each person is experiencing life in their own unique way to learn and to move on the spiral of life. Fear can no longer be generated

149

within us, for we know that our survival is not at risk. Survival of what? We are divine consciousness expressing and no longer have to hold on to anything, since we know that "matter" is energy potential collapsed into particle form. We are divine humans expressing and experiencing in this incarnation as are those individuals being featured by the press. Death of the human body does not end our consciousness. All just is and no longer evokes an addictive dramatic charge.

We also hold love for the family member who is trying to elicit a familiar emotion out of us to play in their drama. With S.T.A.R. wisdom, that family member appears differently to us. We see him or her as an enormous being of light expressing individuated consciousness as an interconnected part of the One Consciousness. As our energy toward that person shifts and has no charge on it, so too will the energy field of that person change to remove itself from or to synchronize with our new expression. We are changing our outer reality by first changing our inner thinking and feeling in the now.

Where else does drama show up? We can site numerous examples, but the solution will be the same. Who are you in each situation? What do you dream? Those are the major issues. To remove drama from our lives, we have to intend to do so individually, then as others observe us as models, it becomes the new collective consciousness, which absolutely creates new ways to be on earth. We will make decisions no longer based on the expectations of the collective consciousness but now from an inner knowing, which will guide us, by means of new choices, into the next perfect experience for expansion of the conscious awareness of who we are.

Are we afraid that an environment of harmony and joy would be a boring existence? Let's ask the questions in a zero point, non-dualistic field of awareness.

 What would a life without drama *look* like?
What would a life without drama *feel* like?
(Clue: There is no drama if we are in the
NOW = play.)

Let the answers come to us from our will connecting with the will of the divine Creator. That is from where we will see, know and feel the answers. When we repeat this process, it changes the chemical connections and unwires the old circuits so that we begin to create that way of being and that behavior, a balanced emotional response to stimuli knowing that whatever we create is always perfect.

What are the impacts of this new collective consciousness on systems? Political campaigns would eventually observe what the voter wants and would respond in kind. Military decisions would be made differently, because again the vote is the controlling factor in the United States and decision makers would change to reflect the choice of the people. Television and movies would have a different focus, because dollars spent would determine the content provided. The legal systems would completely transform. It is all about our new choices and standing as sovereign beings willing to change our actions. Then, as more and more people become aware of their inner power, the power that has controlled them from the outside no longer has impact.

We will move out of the low energy frequencies of fear, blame, shame, anger. By engaging fully in the frequency of love, we will create an external reality that matches those vibrational octaves. The waves of possibility will be collapsed into new particle form by means of merely choosing differently with our will in alignment with the will of the divine Creator.

Drama does not exist in S.T.A.R. when one has surrendered to the tranquility of knowing human divinity, trusted in wholeness to express, allowed human divinity to evolve and received with appreciation and gratitude what wholeness has imagined and chosen.

S.T.A.R. BEYOND DRAMA

When we hold love we can:

Surrender by disengaging from drama

Trust in our ability to maintain the octaves of love

Allow those who wish to continue to engage in
  drama to do so

Receive waves of new possibilities

In this example, each of the Essential Qualities is activated when:

Wholeness (human divinity) chooses to become the
  observer rather than the participant in the drama.

Self-love disconnects us from drama and connects us
  to our divinity.

Play (the now moment) when imagined creates new
  drama-free experiences.

Embodiment of the Expanded Golden Rule creates
  the model of self-love, which affects others'
  ability to exit the drama and practice self-love.

WILLFUL FINANCIAL HEALTH

Finance is the study of how we invest assets over time. The first asset that comes to mind is money. What exactly is money? Is it not just another expression of created reality or collapsed waves of possibility that manifests into form or matter? Wow, then we could imagine it as a coin or a piece of paper with a president's face on it. Or we could go deeper and see it as tiny dots, invisible to the eye, that have come together to create a unit of energy that is expressing as money. So basically, money is a unit of energy, to which we have attributed certain values.

When we think of willful use of this unit of energy, where is the power? Is the power with the piece of paper or coin or is it with the investor of the asset or divine human? Could it be that we, as creator beings, are choosing on all occasions, how we wish to direct (or invest) the energy of money? If there is a flow, we can stop and start that flow at will, consciously or subconsciously. Why would we stop the flow? Perhaps to create an experience?

What I am alluding to is that money is an energy tool, which we command, to create experiences for our personal growth on the spiral of life. When we let the piece of paper or coin define us, we are giving our power away. When we recognize that it is a tool for our creative use, we hold the power. All judgment disappears when we see money as an instrument with which to play.

Is it possible that the homeless person on the street corner chose to incarnate in that unique expression to experience life in that manner? Is it possible that in another incarnation that same soul might have chosen abundant wealth? In my current incarnation, I have chosen both. I can feel now, as I write, my emotions when I fumbled through jacket pockets searching to find just enough coins to place a call to my children. I had to go to a pay phone, located down the street at the local gas station, because my phone service had been disconnected. I can also feel my emotions when I recently loaned a friend enough money to fulfill her dream to be at a specific sacred site on winter solstice, 2012, because I had the resources to assist her.

We are sovereign authors of our reality.

The energy of money flowed differently in both of those two situations. Each experience had an impact on me. I can also feel what it was like to be late in paying my taxes. I can feel what it was like to be able to fly to Egypt and Israel to do ceremony with new friends with ease and grace. I can feel what it was like to lose my primary home. I can feel what it was like to spend more on a gift for someone I cared for than I would normally have done, just because I wanted to.

None of these experiences are my identity. They are experiences that I chose, consciously or subconsciously, to grow in spirit. They are my experiences, and I will not allow my environment to judge me for perceived lack or perceived plenty. The energy of created reality, in the form of currency, is mine to invest over time as I choose. This is true for each one of us. We are not diminished as an enormous being of light because our pockets are either empty or overflowing.

How we relate to empty or overflowing pockets is how we grow in conscious awareness. That is all it is. It just is. We are playing with the illusion of matter to expand our awareness of who we truly are, sovereign beings authoring our reality.

S.T.A.R. FINANCIAL HEALTH

When we are willfully living our wholeness we can:

Surrender our anxiety to the tranquility of our own internal power

Trust the flow of our assets is divinely orchestrated

Allow lack or plenty to express at our command

Receive all life's experiences with inner calm

In this example, each of the Essential Qualities is activated when:

Wholeness (human divinity) runs the show.

Self-love permeates all our dreaming.

Play (the now moment) removes disharmonious emotions.

Embodiment of the Expanded Golden Rule allows for joyful interplay.

TRUE WELL-BEING

The body communicates information to us in numerous ways. Illness and pain are two ways with which we are familiar. They cause us to move out of a subconscious way of being and to pay attention to our body or our environment. Our first reaction is to take or do something that will return us to "normal." Perhaps that normal no longer serves us, and we should begin to allow new solutions to emerge.

S.T.A.R. wisdom allows us to no longer strive to control our environment and our body, but to observe in fascination what is causing the conditions or symptoms that we are experiencing. Is there something out of alignment in how our body is expressing its current experience? Is there a life lesson that is whispering or even shouting at us that we need to learn? Is our personality running the show and overloading our bodies with an ever-increasing supply of chemicals in response to negative thoughts?

The most powerful tool that we have in applying S.T.A.R. wisdom to our well-being, is metacognition. We can observe our condition and make a conscious choice to respond appropriately. We can be a conscious observer of our body, our environment and our thoughts and feelings about the reality in which we are having our current experience. What is serving us, and what is not serving us?

When we begin to ask those questions, then we can react before our body or environment talks to us in shocking ways to get our attention. We are moving into a stage of conscious evolution, where in knowing our sovereignty we can author our future by choice and willful participation instead of through the subconscious, reactive mode fostered by an unbalanced ego.

Is it possible that what we perceive as being in "un-wellness" is the perfect state of being at a precise moment in time on our journey? Might the condition be sending us a message? How many times have we heard or read about situations where a life-threatening illness or event transformed the individual? They grew in consciousness in ways that astounded those around them. Was this a good thing or was it a bad thing? Or perhaps it just was a chosen experience. We might even want to suggest that the state of un-wellness was chosen as an exit door for the individual to pass beyond the physical state of consciousness expressing, to other realms of consciousness expressing. As we grow in awareness of who we truly are, perhaps we will be able to choose to transition without dis-ease, but by the mere ease of choice.

Wisely observe, choose and respond.

Could well-being be all about aware-ness? Could it be a scale? As the observer, we get to look at the scale of our life as we are living it, not after life as Maat did in ancient Egypt, with her scale, measuring the feather and the heart. Can we be proactive if our well-being scale is out of balance? What is our body telling us by means of the symptoms? What do our life-challenging experiences tell us by means of uncomfortable events? When we apply S.T.A.R. wisdom and metacognition, we have the ability to choose different possibilities from the quantum field. We have forgotten this gift or birthright until now. Our perception of well-being then becomes a tool for self-discovery. When well-being is out of perceived balance, we as conscious beings can make a different choice.

S.T.A.R. WELL-BEING

When we give up control we can:

Surrender to knowing everything just is

Trust each moment is perfection expressing perfection

Allow the flow to enrich our experiences

Receive ALL the gifts that present

In this example, each of the Essential Qualities is activated when:

Wholeness (human divinity) communicates in numerous ways.

Self-love nurtures each unique experience.

Play (the now moment) allows for self-discovery.

Embodiment of the Expanded Golden Rule supports us in seeing all expressions of life as sacred.

BELIEF AND COURAGE

Wisdom is knowledge or information that has no emotional charge and has been accepted as personal truth, which allows us to align our will with the will of the divine Creator. When we have accepted information as simply being our truth, it becomes our belief. We have faith in what we believe in, which gives us courage to act on this innate wisdom. When we have faith and courage in octaves of S.T.A.R. and take action, we reprogram our brain and move into a new identity of self. Our power then moves within to reinforce the courage we need to be this new identity.

 One pure, uncharged thought at a time is all we need to shift into the knowing that we are divine humans.

When we repeat that uncharged thought and add another, we begin an inner alchemy process, or ascension process, of raising our frequency. As our belief about who we are changes, so do our actions, because our new belief gives us courage to behave in new ways.

The word courageous has been said about me often. I am surprised when I hear it because I don't think of myself as being courageous. I am simply acting in a manner that I believe comes from my inner wisdom or truth. How can it be otherwise? What might be more appropriate would be to have someone say to me, "I see a new aspect of you being displayed." My actions seem to stem from courage when they are contrasted with the actions of people around me, whose self-identity is masked by their personality.

> Do you believe and have the courage to accept that you are a divine human?

Having made that statement, I am reminded how difficult it was for me to initially take the first action steps of presenting my new identity to the world, so yes, then it took enormous courage because I was a pioneer and was being a model for a new way of thinking, talking and acting. My story begins when in meditation Archangel Metatron told me who I was, "a divine human," and why I was on the planet, "to be of service." Then I heard, "Speak in front of three hundred and fifty people and share this message and give energy sessions to assist others in their transformation."

At the time, I knew myself to be a mother, grandmother and seeker of divine wisdom. I did not know myself as a teacher and multi-dimensional facilitator. How was I to make the transition, and was it really my truth? At the time, I was just beginning to explore the meaning of the S.T.A.R. acronym. It had not yet become my way of living. Intuitively I surrendered and trusted that the answers would come to me about just what my truth was and how to make a shift, should that be my new path.

Sure enough, day by day in lucid dream state, information came to me about what to say and how to do the energy work. Fortunately, the details came to me step by step, so that there was not an energy overload or emotional crisis, as I began to shift who I knew myself to be. There were days when I had to seek the comfort and guidance of my friends to keep me in balance emotionally. There was an innate knowing that what was coming to me was indeed my truth. As this truth became my belief, I was able to take the necessary action steps, which appeared to others and perhaps myself as courage.

On September 9, 2009 (09/09/09) in Arkansas I stood up in front of a room full of strangers. I was wearing a white outfit and an enormous black hat. As the words came out of my mouth, I observed that some of them were actually funny and the audience was laughing. How curious! When I was complete and the hour's presentation was over, I started to leave the room when I noticed a line of people wishing to speak to me. Some were in tears. Too amazing!

The other astounding discovery was that there was actually a surprise drawing by our host, to see who would fill one open slot, to have a session with me. I saw people in sessions every half hour, from seven in the morning until seven in the evening, for three days except the day that I presented. Perhaps this was courageous, but for me, it was just a belief that these were the action steps that I was to take.

Belief and courage occur when one has surrendered to the tranquility of knowing human divinity, trusted in wholeness to express, allowed human divinity to evolve and received with appreciation and gratitude what wholeness has imagined and chosen.

S.T.A.R. BELIEF & COURAGE

When we are following our innate knowing we can:

Surrender any emotional charge from our thoughts

Trust our inner voice to be our truth

Allow our wisdom to guide our actions

Receive miracles that present to support our belief and courage

In this example, each of the Essential Qualities is activated when:

Wholeness (human divinity) expands belief and courage.

Self-love nurtures one's ability to live their truth.

Play (the now moment) means that we need only focus on the action being taken.

Embodiment of the Expanded Golden Rule gives respect to all with whom we choose to play.

RE-VIEWING CHAOS

A positive response to chaos is possible. That positive response occurs when one moves their understanding of reality from belief in material realism to the ideals expressed through quantum physics supported by owning one's divinity. Freedom from the pain caused by chaos occurs when we no longer identify ourselves by means of our environment. Pain can come from how we judge an experience. Chaos cannot disrupt the conscious observer who is fascinated by the possibilities that are available as a result of the particles of possibilities that are stirred to the surface. Identifying ourselves as part of All That Is allows us to ask the question: "Who do I want to become, and how do I want to feel as a result of the current chaos?"

Events no longer define us when we know ourselves to be sovereign. Those events are merely an invitation to create. As part of the One Consciousness of all matter, we can surrender, allow and trust that a new order will appear. We find our power from the knowing of who we truly are, not from the material condition in which we find ourselves. Losing a grand house on the "right" side of town in no way diminishes our self-love and divine wisdom. The chaos is powerless and cannot knock us off balance. It merely is.

In many cases, chaos can be the external reflection of our new inner awareness shifting to allow for an expanded expression of new aspects of our divine self. Current conditions no longer serve us and are being removed and replaced, although abruptly, by a material reality that is in harmony with our new energy field. We do not need to struggle to hold on to status quo, security, safety, nor fear separation because that is no longer who we are. We are redefining ourselves, and as we do so the multi-dimensional field responds.

There is no longer the feeling of guilt that the chaos we are experiencing might impact the lives of others, for we have a clear understanding that the situation is just that, an event for each one to travel through in their unique way on the spiral of life. Love for those individuals is the remedy, not a rescue. We can have love for those who are affected. Love is always appropriate.

The judgment by others during chaos can no longer impact our emotions, for we are guided by our inner compass or divine wisdom, not by the conditioned responses and expectations of others. "You should" is removed from our inner control panel. We live in fascination observing the unfolding of events and our new behavior as they both present. We don't mind what happens.

When the dust settles, we will be a different expression of consciousness. Hardship is the great teacher. We have to find our way and often look deep within for the answers, not outside of ourselves. By asking the questions, "What am I to learn? How am I to feel?" in the timeless now, we have freed our response to the changing condition from negative emotions from the past and fear from the future. We are allowing the multi-dimensional field to provide the answers, which adjusts our identity from who we were to who we choose to be. By means of exploring possibilities and imagining, "How do I want my new conditions to look like? How will I feel in this new environment?" we become part of creation with the divine Creator.

Chaos is observed as part of the illusion when one has surrendered to the tranquility of knowing human divinity, trusted in wholeness to express, allowed human divinity to evolve and received with appreciation and gratitude what wholeness has imagined and chosen.

S.T.A.R. RE-VIEWING CHAOS

When we remember we are perfection we can:

Surrender false identities

Trust our experiences need not be judged

Allow ourselves to be redefined as sovereign beings

Receive the gifts that change offers

In this example, each of the Essential Qualities is activated when:

Wholeness (human divinity) guides our inner compass.

Self-love adjusts our identity from who we were to whom we choose to be.

Play (the now moment) allows the illusion to lose its power.

Embodiment of the Expanded Golden Rule joins us with all of creation as we imagine the new.

EVOLVING BEYOND COMPASSION

How audacious! We have been taught that to hold compassion for another is an enlightened state of being we should aspire to achieve. Well, what occurred to me was; if you are a divine human and I am a divine human would it not be most appropriate to just love you? Where is the fine distinction between compassion and love, about which I am referring? It is fine indeed!

My awareness began to shift as we moved through the end of the recent 26,000-year Galactic Cycle of Time on winter solstice, December 21, 2012, into a new time cycle. A question to myself appeared, "What is different?" One answer was to be found in the action step that follows S.T.A.R.—accept. No longer was I exploring and studying human divinity as a possibility. I had accepted human divinity as a sovereign being. I knew that all of humanity was awakened or in the process of awakening to their sovereignty. The new energies cascading onto the planet from the increasing solar winds were beginning to give me crystalline clarity to choose sovereignty as my way of being.

Everything began to shift in my physical life and in my beliefs about ways of expressing. How was I now to interact with another, who either knew or was on the cusp of remembering their sovereignty? No more teaching. The desire is to empower that divine being's remembering— sovereign being to sovereign being. I began looking at the energy of the words that I was subconsciously using. As I spoke each one, I knew they influenced the field around me and the reality I was choosing to create. Did I dare look deeply at the word "compassion"?

Compassion can be defined as one having a sympathetic awareness of the distress of another, together with a desire to alleviate it. In the moment, I no longer attach the emotion of distress to events, which have become experiences without any emotional charge for me. I no longer desire to alleviate challenges or rescue another, who is also traveling on the spiral of life. The emotion that is most appropriate is love, not compassion. I can love another, who is perceived to be in distress and in need of rescue, while if I have compassion for what they are experiencing, I am giving energy to that which is causing them pain and suffering.

I don't mean that I would stand by passively observing chaos and discord; I would indeed pull a drowning person into the row boat, should that situation arise, and continue to contribute to food banks and clothing drives. The gifts that I now offer when another is "seeking" are tools for self-empowerment. A recent request from a woman, who came to me seeking advice, might be a good way to explain this.

"Thanks so much, Nina, for your lengthy reply! Loved it! Anyway... now I am thinking maybe I should...What are your thoughts? Or maybe I should have... too. I'm pretty new to this...so guidance would be much appreciated. As well, do I wear the pendant all the time? Also, with the meditation DVD, what happens if I open up too quickly? I am reading your book and some of the things you have gone through concern me, as I work five days a week and have employment responsibilities for other people. However, that being said...I am really wanting to 'wake up'!"

I could so easily have given step-by-step "advice." That would have been my style, but no longer. The questions were not about my truth, but about the truth of the "seeker." I can stand as a model, but my greatest gift now, is to share that she does not "need" me. I am, however, available to empower her remembering, her sovereignty and divinity. For me, that response is not compassion but true love.

The words I chose were:

"I love so much your sharing with me. The most important reply that I can give to you is that YOU know all of the answers. Please trust your innate knowing. Deep within, the divinity that you are wants to know your intentions. In response, you will be guided by YOU. S.T.A.R.: surrender your ego to your human divinity, trust, allow and then receive. Everything that you, as a divine human, choose is perfect. Your ego/personality has fear. Hold the intention to move beyond that identity to the enormity that I know you to be. Whatever you, in wholeness, choose is the perfect direction for you on the spiral of life. Perfection expressing perfection! However you choose to 'play' in the illusion we call our current existence will be a perfect choice for you in the now moment on the spiral of life. Thank you sincerely for your enthusiasm and for choosing to come back to the planet!"

The reply I received was, "Thanks Nina, for your response, and for throwing the ball back in my court. What a delight you are!"

Together through this experience, we shared a transcendent remembering of our unique sovereignty. We had the knowing that there was nothing to correct and nothing to fix. We both were exactly where we were supposed to have been, having exactly the experience that we were choosing to have. Everything just was. Love was the chosen emotion, not compassion.

S.T.A.R. BEYOND COMPASSION

When we are in divine relationship with others we can:

Surrender the will to advise

Trust that every being is purely expressing their own octave of divinity in a manner that is perfect

Allow the people we interact with to transcend without judging where they are on their path

Receive liberation from believing we have a responsibility to heal the world and recognize that our only assignment is to love the world

In this example, each of the Essential Qualities is activated when:

Self-love opens opportunities to be in relationship with others, while responding in loving ways beyond our current understanding of the word compassion.

Wholeness (human divinity) once recognized in self and other beings allows us to move beyond rote student-teacher relating.

Play (the now moment) allows one to appreciate the illusion of each experience as they are being created by us, as sovereign beings.

Embodiment of the Expanded Golden Rule means that we understand that compassion can only occur while judging another's experiences as good, bad, beautiful or ugly while loving sees all as perfection expressing perfection.

A NEW OCTAVE OF WISDOM

S.T.A.R. wisdom has taught us that we are interconnected to all creation by means of individuated consciousness, as divine humans. With this innate knowing, we are able to be the observer of our created reality expressing the emotion of love. The events that appear are just that, events, with no power to evoke debilitating emotions, only fascination.

S.T.A.R. wisdom is the seed planted to creatively blossom into the new ways of being on earth, the Golden Age of Divine Love, which will manifest by means of our co-creative dreaming in the multi-dimensional field with our will in alignment with the will of the divine Creator.

S.T.A.R. wisdom allows us to move our conscious awareness to embrace not only different experiences, new ways of being and cultures with diverse expression, but it will allow us to embrace the next leap forward, being planetary, galactic and cosmic citizens.

We must first love ourselves, then we can have love for our neighbor, then peace with other nations. When we are able to express this love for all creation, we will be able to greet our galactic and cosmic neighbors. The moment is now, as the cycles of time are shifting, and Gaia is putting on her mantle of crystalline frequency, to embrace not only humanity and other star seeds on planet earth, but beings from other planets and galaxies and the cosmos. We are to allow earth to join the galactic federation of worlds and the greater cosmic community, which can only be done when we truly know who we are, for then we know who they are. They are us and we are them, and we can say with love in our hearts, "Welcome." Welcome to all our neighbors expressing uniquely within all creation.

AND SO IT IS.

S.T.A.R. WISDOM

When we are in divine relationship with self we can:

Surrender fear of the unknown

Trust that all of creation is a reflection of the divine Creator

Allow relationships with diverse forms of life

Receive love from realms beyond our knowing

In this example, each of the Essential Qualities is activated when:

Wholeness (human divinity) respects all aspects of creation.

Self-love allows appropriate empathy for others.

Play (the now moment) removes judgment of the unknown.

Embodiment of the Expanded Golden Rule fosters expanded community.

LIVE EVERY DAY
AS A SACRED MOMENT

I SURRENDER TO THE PRESENT MOMENT.

This moment is the only one there is, and it is being gifted to us. What are we going to choose to do with it? Will we honor it or will we subconsciously not notice that this precious experience is a gift, which will fill us with feelings. Which feelings do we wish to play with, as we grow on the spiral of life?

Gratitude, appreciation and love are delicious feelings that move us into new octaves of reality. Choose those and become the observer of life being in it, but not of it. Notice that the behavior of others is truly a reflection of ourselves and look in fascination at what we are seeing. Delight that we are not just observing as a robot, but we are reacting to what presents, which causes a feeling to flow through our bodies. This is truly a gift, to feel, and not just to think.

Let us become the conscious observer of each moment and not let it disappear unnoticed. Before we get out of bed, we can acknowledge the material reality that surrounds us, that we created by our choice amongst all possibilities. The sheets, the sounds, the smells, what it feels like to put our feet on the floor: appreciation and gratitude for all of creation. Be in awe that the waves of possibility support us as we put our full weight on the rug!

When the first person appears in our life that day, we can be the observer of that reflection of our self. With fascination, we know there is no predetermined way of approaching that precious moment occurring in the now. How does the appearance of our friend make us feel? Why is that? How does what is being said make us feel? Why is that? What do they both trigger in us? That is all it is, an experience that makes us feel and think a certain way that then causes us to change (or not change) and behave a certain way. Are we raising our awareness of who we are or not?

Holding enormous appreciation and gratitude for that person for all that they have gifted us in just showing up and entering our environment, so that we can have all of these rich experiences, is precious. Even the negative thoughts and emotions are precious, for that is all they are. Could those negative emotions, that might appear, stir memories within us for us to play with and to discover from where they came? Could they be a catalyst for growth? What a gift our friend has given us, since it has nothing to do with our friend. It is all about us and our growth in conscious awareness of who WE are.

Each moment is precious and a gift to be consciously received and played with. It has no more power than that. We are one with all that presents. To be fully present, focused and aware is to receive with appreciation and gratitude what wholeness has imagined and dreamed. We can then accept what has presented and know we, as sovereign beings, authored this reality from the field of all possibilities, in alignment with the divine Creator.

Thank you for playing with me in the dreaming of our new reality. As we place the mantle of our sovereignty on the temple that is our human body, we are beginning to remember the glorious being that we are and *always* have been and always will be for eternity. We together have begun to imagine new ways of being on earth, the Golden Age of Divine Love, by means of each word read and the energy contained within.

We are invited to continue this journey on the spiral of life as individuated consciousness, in alignment with All That Is. The One Consciousness is who we are. Our ego/personality in perfect balance with our human divinity, is now how we are expressing.

WITH THIS WISDOM FIRMLY INTEGRATED, WE CAN DANCE
THROUGH THE MAYA OF LIFE WITH EASE AND GRACE
KNOWING THAT WE ARE THE AUTHORS OF OUR REALITY,
AND THAT WE NOW TAKE RESPONSIBILITY FOR ALL THAT
WE CREATE.

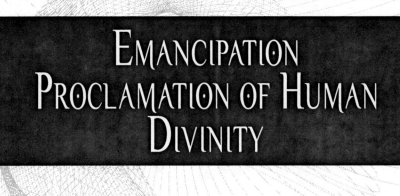

EMANCIPATION PROCLAMATION OF HUMAN DIVINITY

(to be spoken aloud for vibrational attunement)

THE PASSION OF MY SOUL IS TO ACCEPT MYSELF
AS A DIVINE HUMAN, AND FROM THAT WHOLENESS
TO CREATE MY EXPERIENCE.

I proclaim to be free of all limitations imposed from knowing myself as less than whole. I NOW proclaim my soul has returned to its ORIGINAL NATURE.

I NOW reclaim my DIVINE DISCERNMENT to create my reality in all time-frames and dimensions.

I acknowledge I am the divine Creator in human form and hold a frequency from which I emit, that creates the structure of my personal experience. The resonant frequency that I am willing to *receive* is in harmonic resonance with the frequency I am creating.

I proclaim the requisite foundation to support the blooming of the octaves of S.T.A.R. I imagine four foundational pillars, which will anchor me firmly in this new paradigm of knowing that I am All That Is. I require that each pillar be secure to avoid imbalance. I imagine that the first pillar represents the full expression, acceptance and declaration of my human divinity. The second pillar represents the full expression, acceptance and declaration of self-love.

The third pillar represents living in the now moment (the definition of play). The fourth pillar represents living the Expanded Golden Rule — "Do unto all creation as I would have all of creation do unto me."

I proclaim that from this foundation, I will employ the philosophy of S.T.A.R. (surrender, trust, allow, receive) to assist me in expressing and evolving, and that I will receive all that my human divinity has imagined and dreamed with appreciation and gratitude.

I accept the responsibility to radiate love and light and to participate in the Law of Life: life is granted in exchange for light gifted to the cosmos. In so doing, I assist earth in being in balance with all creation.

I proclaim myself free to be all that I am, and that from my divine self, I will now create the shining life I want, the new ways to be on earth and all that I ever dreamed of and beyond.

I accept that I am interconnected with all of creation expressing as individuated consciousness, and with that knowing, I will respect all unique expressions of All That Is.

By means of this EMANCIPATION PROCLAMATION OF HUMAN DIVINITY, I declare that I returned to earth at this time in human evolution to assist others in knowing their sovereignty, so that together we will create, anchor, seed, nurture and grow the Golden Age of Divine Love.

AND SO IT IS.

I know who you
are — you are an
expansive, radiant,
divine being!

GLOSSARY

Adobe: a natural building material made from sand, clay, water, and some kind of fibrous or organic material (sticks, straw, and/or manure).

Akashic record: a compendium of mystical knowledge encoded in a non-physical plane of existence.

Attunement: a harmonious or responsive relationship.

Awareness: conscious connection with universal intelligence. (Tolle)

Being: unconscious thoughts, behavior and feelings.

Carmelite nun: a member of a congregation of Roman Catholic women in the Carmelite (primarily cloistered) tradition, a religious order founded in the 12th century and with a spiritual focus on contemplative prayer.

Cerebellum: the most active part of the brain, located at the back of the skull. The seat of the subconscious.

Clairaudient: the power or faculty of hearing something not present to the ear but regarded as having objective reality.

Collaboration: to work jointly with others or together.

Collapse (quantum physics): the change from possibility into actuality. (Goswami)

Consciousness: the organizing principle behind the arising of form at which point it becomes unconscious of itself: the descent of the divine into matter. (Tolle)

Correlated: to be in a parallel relationship.

Dimension, expanded: now time awareness, which is added to length, breadth and depth of space.

Dimension, third: a dual mode of perception consisting of length, breadth and depth of space. A dense version of consciousness. A reality of rigid beliefs, with a relatively inflexible set of rules and limitations. No possibility of choice, we don't choose our thoughts, feelings, and actions in every moment (that's a skill of 4D and 5D), instead we react from unconscious beliefs and training to the people and situations that pop up in our space.

Dimension, multi-: states of consciousness available to anyone who vibrates in resonance with the specific frequencies and opportunities available within each dimension. There are differing sciences, different physics for each dimension. Dimensional planes do not occupy space.

Discernment: the quality of being able to grasp and comprehend what is obscure.

Divine: the state of things that come from a supernatural power or deity, such as God, and are therefore regarded as sacred and holy. Such things are regarded as "divine" due to their transcendental origins.

Divine will: the heart/mind faculty by which wholeness deliberately chooses or decides upon a course of action.

eBay: an online shopping and auction network.

Ego: the part of the mind that believes it is separate from the consciousness of the divine Creator. The personality identification with individual existence.

Eight Northern Pueblos: a council of the eight sovereign Indian tribes which lie between Santa Fe and Colorado.

Emancipation: the act or process of freeing.

Energy, new: the massive injection of cosmic radiation on the planet from solar winds.

Expanded Golden Rule: the Golden Rule is limited to the interaction between humans. Its expanded state encompasses the interaction of all creation. "Do unto all of creation, what we would have all of creation do unto us."

Four pillars: author's visualization for four principles which, when mastered, serve as structural foundation for S.T.A.R. These are: human divinity, self-love, play and the Expanded Golden Rule.

Forum, The Landmark: the flagship program of Landmark Education developed to permanently shift the quality of one's life in just three days. The work is based on the est training (Erhard Seminars Training) developed by Werner Erhard.

Frequency: the number of cycles per second. It's the measure of how fast a wave wiggles. For light, that means color: White light is made up of light of various frequencies, or colors. Red is low-frequency light, and violet is high-frequency light. If the frequency is even higher, it's invisible black light, what we call ultraviolet. (Goswami)

Golden Age of Divine Love: the new earth, a shift in dimensional reality.

Harmonic: a discrete spectrum of frequencies (series of sounds) expressed as stationary waves along a line. The lowest sound is called the first harmonic, which determines pitch. The higher musical sounds in the note are the quality.

Human, divine: divine Creator in human flesh. An extension of the One Consciousness.

Indian Pueblo Cultural Center: gateway to the nineteen Indian Pueblos in New Mexico.

Infinity, the space of: space between the particles of creation.

Inner compass: one's intuition or innate knowing.

Innocent perception: to be aware without bias.

Intention: thought or electrical impulse for manifestation.

Joy: an expanded state of happiness approaching bliss (emanation of the frequency of love). An emotion with a high vibration.

Kindness: the expression of the Expanded Golden Rule.

Landmark Education: a global educational enterprise offering training in personal development.

Law of resonance: when one vibrating system (physical body) comes into contact with another vibrating system (another physical body), the vibration of the weaker body will adjust its energy to match that of the stronger body. In other words, the vibration of the stronger system will adjust the energy of the weaker system.

Limbic brain: the most highly developed and specialized area of the brain located under the neocortex. The emotional brain is responsible for the manufacturing and secretion of chemicals in the form of peptides.

Magic: the divine human's command of the unified energy field by means of choice.

Manifestation: materialization, a possibility which comes into perceptible existence, appears, becomes actual or real.

Material realism: a belief that mind and matter are divided.

Maya: an illusion centered on the fact that we do not experience the environment itself but rather a projection of it, created by us.

Metacognition: one's knowledge concerning one's own cognitive processes or anything related to them.

My Original God Tone: the frequency of the divine Creator which resides in our sacred heart, which has been forgotten by our ego/personality.

Neocortex: our "thinking brain" or walnut-like outer covering, which is the seat of the conscious mind, our identity, and other higher brain functions. (Dispenza)

Neuropeptide: any of several types of molecules found in brain tissue, composed of short chains of amino acids including endorphins, enkephalins, vasopressin, and others.

Neurosensory diagnostic equipment: a medical device developed by Neurosensory Centers of America, which tests and provides a graphical analysis of one's Neurosensory system, so a physician can "see" and treat the source of the problem. www.neurosensorycenters.com

Now: only the present moment, with no emotional charge from the past or the future.

Now moment: play.

Now ways of being on earth: the transcendence of an ego-based state of consciousness to the awakening of a new state of oneness-based, unity consciousness, and its reflection in the physical realm.

Octave: a musical interval consisting of eight diatonic (musical scale with intervals of five whole steps and two half steps) degrees. With S.T.A.R., octaves are non-hierarchal frequencies of energy carrying incorruptible data that are ascending or descending based upon the recipient's ability to receive, assimilate or integrate what is offered within that specific octave.

Octaves of light: see octave.

Personality: identity of ego self.

Philosophy: the activity through which we see creation through the eyes of the Creator. The full octave expression of philosophy is about nurturing the seeds of wisdom hibernating in our sacred hearts. We are born with those seeds. The philosopher's stone, that holds the secret seeds to everything, has transformed into the philosopher's seed—a living being which can burst forth into new, never before expressed shapes, forms with playful creativity.

Physics, quantum: a branch of science that deals with discrete, indivisible units of energy.

Pio, Padre: Saint Pio (Pius) of Pietrelcina, O.F.M. Cap., (May 25, 1887 – September 23, 1968) was a Capuchin Catholic priest from Italy who is venerated as a saint in the Catholic Church.

Play: the now moment. Any activity, business or pleasure that is experienced unrestricted by suffering from the past or fear of the future.

Quantum (plural: quanta): the minimum unit (amount) of any physical entity involved in an interaction (physics).

Quantum field: invisible potential energy that is able to organize itself from energy to subatomic particles to atoms to molecules, and on up the line to everything. (Dispenza)

Quantum field: see unified (energy) field.

Quantum leap: movement of a thing in a disjointed or discontinuous manner, jumping from one place to another, seemingly without effort and without bothering to go between the two places. Classical physics has objects move in a flow from one point to another. (Fred Alan Wolf)

Quantum physics: a physical science that was developed to explain the nature and behavior of matter and energy on the scale of atoms and subatomic particles, but now is believed to hold true for all matter (even galaxies). (Goswami)

Reality, possible: possibilities of consciousness itself, which is the ground of all being. Our looking is tantamount to choosing from among the quantum possibilities the one unique facet that becomes our experienced actuality. (Goswami)

S.T.A.R.: acronym for surrender, trust, allow and receive.

S.T.A.R. clinic: a multi-dimensional tool to assist one in awakening to their human divinity, based on the philosophies of surrender, trust, allow and receive.

Sacred heart: the center of one's soul; the point of oneness with Source.

Self-love: genuine love of self that often begins with the knowing that one is an individual aspect of All That Is and perfect in all forms of that expression.

Spiral of life: a concept which implies the soul's growth and expansion.

Spiritual strength: the resolve that one's innate wisdom is aligned with the will of the divine Creator.

Sovereign being: when there is no higher authority than one's innate knowing within.

Sovereignty: the act of being one's own authority.

State of being: when mind and body are one.

Synchronicity: an apparently meaningful coincidence in time of two or more similar or identical events that are causally unrelated.

Transcendent: extending or lying beyond the limits of all possible experience and knowledge, being beyond comprehension. (Goswami)

Unified (energy) field: a type of field theory that allows all that is usually thought of as fundamental forces and elementary particles to be written in terms of a single field.

Voice, inner: a cellular intelligence that one has inside, that often stands apart from you, but which knows you. What you trust when you decide to do things such as muscle testing and kinesiology.

Waves of Possibility: quantum physics term describing discrete non-localized energy units which can occupy any region of space and then collapse into any localized particle form.

Wholeness: the state of being one's human divinity.

Wisdom: a state of being wise; integration of knowledge, experience and deep understanding. A memory without the emotional charge. (Dispenza)

Zero point: a non-magnetic plane.

Author's Statement to the Universe

My intention has been to share with the utmost clarity my understanding of the S.T.A.R. philosophy.

S.T.A.R. was given to me through James F. Jereb. I accepted this gift and deeply experimented with it in my own life. I can now see that the reason was so I could communicate this wisdom to others.

Having done so in this book, I have chosen not to contain, possess, horde or own S.T.A.R. It belongs to all of humanity. Therefore, I choose to let it out into the cosmos to go where it wishes.

My desire is that many other people will start to experiment with the S.T.A.R. philosophy in their own lives. At this time, there is no certification process for teachers or practitioners, yet there are many people who have already started to practice these concepts with amazing results. Perhaps in the future these people will also choose to write books or do new things that I never imagined with S.T.A.R. I will not review, approve and/or scrutinize these books. For those who might choose to work with or read additional books about S.T.A.R. from other people sharing what they have learned, my suggestion is to see if the material resonates with you through choosing to use your own personal discernment and inner guidance.

ABOUT THE AUTHOR

Nina Brown, a nontraditionally aged cum laude graduate of Bryn Mawr College, went on to distinguish herself as a pioneer in business. In 1990, she established an investment company to assist women entrepreneurs. In 1995, she was appointed by President Bill Clinton to represent him at the White House Conference on Small Business and, the next year, was chosen as a Charter Member of Pennsylvania's Best 50 Women in Business. During this time, she presented at speaking engagements hosted by the US House of Representatives Field Hearings, the Pennsylvania Department of Commerce, the League of Cities Women's Caucus, Wharton Executive MBA Reunion and the Entrepreneurial Women's Expo, where she was the keynote speaker.

Nina subsequently became a consultant and leader in alternative medicine. Among other initiatives, she collaborated in forming a company to bring neurosensory diagnostic tools to injured veterans who suffered brain impairment in the Gulf and Vietnam Wars.

In 2014, after the publication of *S.T.A.R. Philosophy*, she traveled to India, where she presented before a gathering of more than 2,000 members of the Pyramid Society of Spiritual Scientists. While in India, she took S.T.A.R. philosophy to Raipur and Mumbai, and then on to Singapore. Two years later, Life University (http://lu-global.org/about-us/) in India asked to add *S.T.A.R. Philosophy* and its companion book, *The Fascinated Observer: A Guide to Embodying S.T.A.R. Philosophy*, to its curriculum.

Currently Nina serves on the executive board of Pristina Natural, Inc., helping to expand the company's presence across the United States and into Canada and Asia. Her desire is to bring S.T.A.R.

philosophy into the realm of business, creating a new model for the union of consciousness and business.

Throughout her endeavors, she has been guided by S.T.A.R. principles, devoting her energies full-time to this sacred spiritual mission. She has found that as the needs of the collective shift, the service asked of her evolves, and this transformative work unfolds.

In addition to writing the S.T.A.R. series, Nina is the author of *Return of Love to Planet Earth: Memoir of a Reluctant Visionary.* Her writing has also been published in *Kindred Spirit* and *Sedona Journal of Emergence.*

ORDERING INFORMATION

Nina Brown's other books are also available through select bookstores, online retailers, and CaudaPavonisPub.com, which also offers quantity discounts for bulk purchases.

RETURN OF LOVE TO PLANET EARTH
Memoir of a Reluctant Visionary

6" x 9"
978-0-9826769-0-5
388 pages
$19.95
eBook: $9.99

INDIE EXCELLENCE FINALIST
USA BEST BOOK AWARDS FINALIST

"What a treat to be privy to the journey of a walking master one who has successfully assimilated all aspects of her higher self."
—Dr. Bali K. Sohi, psychologist

"A must-read for any spiritual seeker."
—Lee Carroll

"In reading this beautiful book you will gain a deeper appreciation for your own life and a greater understanding of who you really are."
—Robert Schwartz, author of *Your Soul's Plan*

S.T.A.R. Series ~ Book 2
THE FASCINATED OBSERVER
A Guide to Embodying S.T.A.R. Philosophy

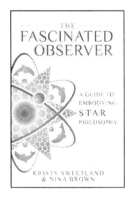

6" x 9"
978-0-9826769-3-6
250 pages
$17.00
eBook: $9.99

"Kristy and Nina have created a powerful encouragement, a wave of energy that will carry you closer to your true self."
—**David Bedrick, JD, Dipl PW, author of**
Talking Back to Dr. Phil

"For those who desire greater richness, insight and...renewed fascination with the wonders of everyday magical possibilities."
—**Cheryl Eckl, author of** *The Light Process*

"This book paves an avenue for us to develop into reflective, observant, awake and aware fascinating beings serving our souls and our communities."
—**Patty Hlava, PhD, Midwest Meditation and**
Psychotherapy Institute

Cauda Pavonis
PO Box 32445
Santa Fe, New Mexico 87594
CaudaPavonisPub.com

CPSIA information can be obtained
at www.ICGtesting.com
Printed in the USA
FFOW04n1807130418
46232840-47589FF

9 780982 676912